'Keith is certainly
audacity an

Arsène Wenger
Former Arsenal Manager and FIFA Global Head of Football Development

COJONES

GROW A PAIR FOR SUCCESS!

KEITH G FRASER

Cojones

First published in 2020 by

Panoma Press Ltd
48 St Vincent Drive, St Albans, Herts, AL1 5SJ, UK
info@panomapress.com
www.panomapress.com

Book layout by Neil Coe.

978-1-784529-22-2

The right of Keith G Fraser to be identified as the author of this work has been asserted in accordance with sections 77 and 78 of the Copyright, Designs and Patents Act 1988.

A CIP catalogue record for this book is available from the British Library.

This book is available online and in bookstores.

Dear Maria,
I hope you like the book!
Here's to working with you
soon.
All the best,

DEDICATION

To my late father Gerald Fraser, who died 14th May 1985.
A man of real bravery, whose suffering and its impact on me
has undoubtedly fuelled this project.

And

To my son Rafael who I'd love to heed some of this book's
messages in shaping his life, and of course my wife Amira, whose
continuing encouragement has enabled me to complete it finally!

TESTIMONIALS

"This book is not for someone who is comfortable sitting on the fence. It is directly in your face opinions, some of which you will not necessarily agree with. Above all it is an honest assessment of what it takes to make your way in an often difficult and sometimes cruel world."

Barry Hearn, legendary Founder of Matchroom Sport and the UK's Number 1 Sports Promoter and Entrepreneur

"Keith is certainly true to his message of audacity and perseverance - two vital ingredients of success."

Arsène Wenger, Arsenal Football Club's greatest ever Manager and FIFA Global Head of Football Development

"A fascinating analysis of a vital subject."

Alastair Campbell, former Spokesman and Strategist to UK Prime Minister, Tony Blair

"Keith Fraser would give Ben Stokes a run for his money: he is a true all-rounder.

A talented salesman, speaker and motivator, Keith is someone with great gifts and great stories which make this book such a great read. Not only are his stories inspiring but the tools he describes are effective and easy to put into practice. The first of many Keith Fraser books, I do hope."

Gary Leboff, The UK's Number 1 Performance Psychologist

"This book is what it says on the tin; not just another self-help book. Fraser gives us a well-researched, psychologically well-informed, captivating approach to a new way of thinking about your feelings, behaviours and life patterns. Fuelled by coherent insights from his own and other's journeys, he gives us the tools to use as we see fit to become the architects of our own lives."

Dr Shelley Gilbert MBE, PhD, PGDPM, PGDC, Snr Accredited MBACP

Founder & President of Grief Encounter (The Child Bereavement Charity)

ACKNOWLEDGEMENTS

This is often the part of the book that's a tad boring for people to read, as it's so personal and of course, you don't know the individuals being referred to. So I am going to keep it brief and tell you why I wanted to pay special homage to these people, and hopefully it will help to provide further insights into the whole book itself.

Without wishing to sound clichéd, my mother always said that behind every successful man is a good woman. My cynical self used to answer, "Yes... behind."

I have to tell you that there are only a few people in my life who have really fuelled this journey, and the main one is my wife Amira. I would never have done it without her. She has always believed in me when at times I haven't truly believed in myself. She has always told me I could do it when at the back of my mind I wasn't always sure. And not just because she is my wife, she has always truly believed I have the capabilities, and I am very lucky and grateful.

Of course, one of the reasons I wanted to put some of my learnings and teachings down into a book is so that my beautiful son, when he's old enough, will be able to pick it up and read. I really hope he can live his life authentically, with his dreams he will have the belief he can fulfil them. I therefore have to thank him even if he wouldn't realise at the time of writing why he is also a catalyst for me 'putting pen to paper'.

My friend and long-term mentor Gary Leboff has to be mentioned. He has become a friend and someone who knows me, my talents and Achilles' heels only too well. He has always been extremely supportive and has continually put the seeds of 'can do' in my mind. Gary has incredible intuition and I have always trusted his judgment and advice. Gary, I could not have done this without you.

I'd also like to say thank you to the incredible Mavis Klein, who is unfortunately not alive to read this piece of work or see my development. Whilst I proved to be a difficult student of her theories and healing strategies, she was one of the most interesting and intelligent people I have ever met. That chance meeting in the coffee shop when she overheard my conversation on psychology and astrology, when she turned around and slapped her marketing leaflet on my table, was a moment of divine intervention. Learning Transactional Analysis from her, the best, and loads more, is something I am forever grateful for. Thanks Mavis.

Ian Watson deserves a mention. He taught me loads on the Three Principles, which is so relevant to much of what I talk about in this book. Thanks for the wisdom Ian.

I have to mention a few of my close friends who have also believed in me, and been particularly encouraging, for which I am also very grateful. Encourage is to my mind 'to give courage' and we all need that from time to time, so here are just a few.

Francis Hill, what an amazing sounding board you've been. I'm hugely grateful to you.

Andy Moss. A friend I never see but I can honestly say that his kindness and belief in me has always been appreciated. I have no idea why, but he has always supported me and indeed motivated me. Thanks Andy. Be good to see you some time.

My close friends Jon and Chris also. I'm not sure they totally understand the crux of this book, despite me explaining many, many times. Hopefully, when I give them a free copy they'll get the drift. I am thankful for their friendship, and particularly Jon for his support and encouragement.

There's also Daniel, who is always there to support me and come to some of my events. I am thankful for his steadfast loyalty. Louis Bloom and Lloyd Millett too, who are again loyal but very encouraging, and who have shown to only want good things for me.

My mother, whilst not always seeing eye to eye with me, has also been someone who through enormous difficulties in life has somehow managed to get through them. Without even realising it, she is, and has been, unbelievably strong whilst not always being dealt a fair hand. Everyone could learn from her resolve. I know I certainly have.

If I have missed anyone out, and I can already think of a few, I apologise, but this book has been in abeyance for so long I just want to get it done now.

If I have left you out, do let me know, and if I think you should have been here, I'll be more than apologetic. If not, you know what you can do.

All the above though, in some form or another, have had a huge impact on me. Without learning lessons from them, receiving encouragement, and feeling their genuine support, I could never have done this. Thank you again.

Hope you guys, and especially the readers, enjoy the book and gain something from it.

Keith Fraser

October 2020

CONTENTS

INTRODUCTION

"The universe applauds action not thought."

Anon

Respect goes to you for picking up this book. Why? Because hopefully you will have already realised that you want to be different, do things differently and simply go for it. You obviously realise that actually, up 'til now, you've lacked a pair, and what you want in order to move forward is to 'grow a pair', yes, a pair of balls, or as my famous brand calls it… Cojones.

If you are in the slightest bit offended by the title or notion of this book, and even the first paragraph above, then you need to do one of two things: 1) either go and read Miss Marple or something, or 2) lighten up, let the shackles go and realise that you need to use what you have to enjoy a full and proper life.

Above I've included a saying that I picked up from a personal development course I did many moons ago. Probably the only thing I picked up, but useful at least. You've probably heard this saying before, and if not, nothing could be nearer to the truth in terms of evolution, moving forward and growth, both in the world as a whole and as an individual.

If you have ever taken a look at my website, and if not it's about time you did, you will see that I am not too complimentary about the personal development field, as on the whole, in my eyes, it encourages delusion and gives false hope to people. Don't get me wrong, if you get something out of it, then that's great, and of course the one message that is a good one is that positivity and self-belief are vital, because indeed they are.

But what positivity and self-belief won't give you on their own are results, success, or achievement, depending on how you define it. The only thing that counts when it comes to moving forward with yourself, your quest for a good job, a business, a healthy relationship or whatever, is action, hence why I pay homage to the one message I learned years ago on that course.

I know all the self-help junkies will be insulted or disappointed with what I say, and that's tough, but I know, as I used to be one, so I can tell you the reality. From experience I can tell you categorically that you can read every title on the shelf, but it'll make little difference without the single most important tenet, and one that I have underlined – Cojones. You see, I am the first person to identify that the one factor in any walk of life's achievement that really counts is having a pair of balls. For both men and women.

On the whole, we live in a pathetically weak society now, in which the fastest growing religion is Political Correctness. As you will see later in the chapter about the Ten Commandments of Cojones, political correctness is simply lying, but because people are now so scared to offend for fear of being derided, and even losing one's job, we remain quiet and our opinions are kept to ourselves. Cojones overcomes this horrible modern religion and yes, so much more, as you will see.

This book is about the theory and practice of the one single ingredient that makes the world and people move.

Cojones is the Spanish slang for balls, and whilst Mary Whitehouse fans may be insulted by that, if you want to have a great life in which you live life to the max, achieve to the best of your abilities, then you need to learn how to embrace Cojones.

Only the other day when I was over at a friend's house, his son, who is close to obtaining his Shotokan Karate black belt, was too self-conscious to show me some of what he learns. It wasn't shyness, it was fear of judgment, which is why so many have no Cojones, yet this premise applies to everything.

How many times have you wanted to ask someone for a date, ask for their number, phone a CEO to get some advice, or see if there's a job going, or simply put yourself forward for anything and not done so because you didn't have the balls?

The list is endless, with everyone, and it feels horrid doesn't it? The saying 'When you look back, you'll regret much more what you haven't done than what you have' is so, so true, but if you had grown a pair at the time you 'bottled it', as well as at other times, you wouldn't feel so much regret I can assure you.

Well, this is what this book is about. It's about taking action, overthinking less, saying what you feel, approaching anyone, thinking outside the box, and feeling great about doing it. With Cojones you will see that things you never would have dared do before are doable, or at least tryable, and you'll have fun along the way.

If you want me to tell you a Bentley or Ferrari is on the way, just from thinking it, then go to the thousands of other titles in the personal development section of your local bookshop, as you won't get it here. I will tell you as it is, and outline that fearless action and boldness is what's required, and how to embrace it.

Get ready to read a book that is straight talking and no nonsense. I am not going to make promises that you will be a new person, as that's down to you, and only you, and is your problem if you don't heed my words; but if you do, then I can tell you, you will be well on your way.

I am a lover of quotes and they say 'God helps those who help themselves.' Well maybe, but I say instead, "If you really want to help yourself, and have decided to do so, then help is all around you."

So, if you've taken that important decision, and are willing to do it, then read on. But if you're not, go somewhere else and enjoy being in your shell, 'cos this book won't be for you.

CHAPTER 1:

WHY THE WORLD NEEDS COJONES... BADLY!

You may think that's a bit of a statement. Well I don't. In my eyes, if we all lived by the Cojones Code to some degree at least, we'd all be a bit happier, live more authentically and no longer be victims.

Now I know what being a victim is and I think many people do. I've played the victim a lot in my life – the thing is, it was only fairly recently that I realised that I was playing it!

I mentioned that I studied in some depth the wonderful psychological language of Transactional Analysis. One of the most famous books on this subject is written by its founder Eric Berne, called *Games People Play*, and one of the things it tells you is that we adopt roles and play games, including that of victim, without even knowing. If you do want to read in greater depth on this subject, I highly recommend that book, as I strongly believe that if you have any understanding of the subject, you will have a greater understanding of yourself, allowing you to make changes to your ways and default behaviour.

Anyway, as I said, the world to my mind needs Cojones, and badly. NOW!!

First off, anyone who is anyone who has achieved anything will have demonstrated Cojones to do so in some shape or form. Whether you are starting a business, asking a woman to marry you (or asking a man to marry you), performing on stage, giving a business pitch, standing for election, entering a sports tournament, literally anything you can think of, takes an element of Cojones.

Of course, if you want to be a Cojones Icon, as I will highlight later in this book, you will need to show 'super Cojones', but of course not everyone can be like them. We can though, as we have seen, learn from them by adopting some of their qualities and traits.

But, let's take success out of it for now, because 'success' is a very subjective word. To my mind, if you are a contented happy person, then you're a successful person, and if you adopt the Cojones Code you will be going some way towards that.

If you need any convincing why you should be reading this book, then hopefully this chapter will resonate with you, and at the end you will be saying to yourself 'I see what you mean Keith'.

You see, sadly we are living in a generation where increasing numbers of people are simply gutless, let alone Cojones-less. This book is all about taking back control (I sound like a Brexit politician). That's right, truly living in a free society.

So what about Cojones in society, and life itself? Let's look at some of life's and society's norms to understand why we need Cojones.

Home life

Are you a doormat or a doorbell? What I mean is, are you a yes man or woman who's walked all over by their partner or spouse, or do you ring the bell and call the tune? Actually if you say you're the latter, then the likelihood is that your partner is the doormat, so that's wrong too, but if you are a doormat, then why? Why do you think, act and behave like you are so unimportant?

I have a dear friend, a woman, who sadly had a terrible marriage. A husband who had no sense of duty to her or his family. Too lazy to work and provide for his family, cheated on his wife, etc, etc. This man, who incessantly claims poverty, is still on the phone to his ex-wife (they are divorced now) to ask for money. He has some cheek. But wait for it… she gives it to him.

It's interesting that (particularly women – sorry, ladies) when females meet for coffee, the main topic of conversation is complaining about their men. If they aren't treating you with the respect you deserve as a fellow human being, then start to grow a pair and stick up for yourself and maintain some self-respect. Stop moaning for heaven's sake, as one of the Cojones Ten Commandments will tell you.

In your home life, there should be some equality, not someone wearing the trousers as they say, and if you are not in an equal relationship, then either adopt the Cojones Code or get out of the relationship. Life's too short, isn't it?

Yeah I know, it takes Cojones to get out too, but I don't have the time to cover that as well.

What about kids if you have them? Are you a parental pushover? Then shame on you. No wonder all kids seem to have everything they want – NOW.

When I grew up, my parents were parents. I hear it a lot on radio from people: "Oh my daughter's my best friend." Hogwash. You're her parent, and you will gain respect for being so.

I never forget being told some wise words of advice about parenthood – the three Fs: Fun, Fair and Firm. That means be strict when you need to, so as to instil good values and manners, but be fair, always. So, don't be strict and over exertive of your own will for the sake of it, and of course, don't forget to be fun.

It's tough today, isn't it? My five-year-old wants a games console like all of his school friends. He hasn't got one at the moment. Why? Games consoles and the games or software are very expensive. He will have to wait, and may even have to contribute with his own pocket money. What kind of values would I be teaching him if I laid out a few hundred pounds just like that? I don't want him to feel a sense of lack, where everyone has and he hasn't, but come on, I want him to learn the value of money and to understand that we can't have everything we demand in an instant.

If more parents had the balls to stand up for the same moral code, then perhaps people and the country wouldn't be in so much financial debt. Parents need Cojones too.

When your kids are in teenhood they will respect you in the future if you follow the above three Fs. If you are a pushover, your kids will end up like the rest of today's society: lazy and whiney, annoyed that the world doesn't revolve around them, whilst expectant of everything, without doing anything to earn it.

Work

Now here is a context in which you need to adopt the Cojones Code. If you are a boss, if you are an employer, if you are an employee, if you are a team leader, or whatever title you may hold.

If you are the boss you will likely have already applied some Cojones to be one, but whilst you are one you will need to take some important decisions, whether that be whom you employ, whom you fire, whom you give a kick up the arse, and all the facets that running a business entails.

If you are an employee, if you work hard and do your job well, you should stand proud and expect respect and appreciation, whether you're paid a fortune or not. Cojones will enable you to ensure you have self-respect. If you are treated unfairly, say so. Don't be a coward. But don't be a victim either.

Yes, you may well deserve respect and appreciation, but if you are needy and a perennial victim, then you are setting yourself up to be picked on, and will likely receive the opposite. You see, bullying is commonplace, not just in schools. It is rife in the workplace as well, with office politics too often spoiling the work life and productivity of many.

It is important to have the strength not to get sucked into the tittle-tattle. You must learn to rise above that nonsense. But, and here's the big BUT, if you are being talked about badly, spoken to disrespectfully, for heaven's sake stand up and grow a pair!

A good friend of my wife was literally bullied by her boss to the point of abuse. While she was in the job she was afraid to stand up for herself, such was her low self-esteem. Naturally she was very unhappy. She was literally petrified of her boss who was a cowardly bully. But this lady was afraid of unsettling the status quo of her co-workers as they also took no action, such was their mutual fear of losing their job.

The fascinating thing is, this lady, in her new job, has also been bullied by her new boss. Bottom line is – she asks for it.

Now before you start to get angry with what I just said, of course no one deserves to be treated like that, but bullies seek out people who by default play the victim. They need the weak. But of course, if you had any Cojones you would no longer be a victim, and bullies wouldn't seek you out.

So, at work too, you need to adopt the Cojones Code.

Society

As you will find out later, one of the Cojones Ten Commandments, my codes for living with Cojones for an authentic and successful life, is End Political Correctness.

We live in such a sanitised society. We can't do or say anything without offending someone, who'll then demand an apology. It has simply got way out of hand. There are limits and boundaries, but nowadays we all have to walk on eggshells so that we don't offend.

Possibly the greatest British comedy sitcom ever, *Only Fools and Horses*, would likely not be allowed to be commissioned today, due to its non-politically correct script. Yet, it is loved by the majority of the country. What's happened to a good old sense of humour?

I mention later in the book the Yiddish word *chutzpah*. Another area the Jewish community is known for is comedy. Look at numerous sitcoms in the US and you'll find a swathe of Jewish writers. Why?

Well, not only are Jewish people rather neurotic but they are also self-deprecating. Yes, aware of their neurosis, and not afraid of mocking it, ie not taking themselves too seriously.

So why is the world so way oversensitive? Loosen up, get a life and grow a pair!

Humour is often the best way to learn, and when I talk to an audience I aim for people to learn through laughter. My brand and logo (yes you've guessed it, Cojones), whilst being slightly tongue-in-cheek and meant to be somewhat humorous, has a serious message as you will have noticed reading this book. The logo is of course a spin on a pair of testicles, or balls. But, at the same time, it's in no way meant to be, nor is, sexist. On the contrary, if anyone should be offended by it, it should be men, as it mocks a body part of our gender.

Cojones is a mindset. One for men and women to adopt. Yet you would not be surprised to hear that some people have occasionally cancelled my talks as they think it could be construed as offensive or sexist in some way. What tosh! Actually, in relation to Cojones... what a load of utter bollocks! Oops, does that offend you? Good. Get used to it. Cojones is about saying it how it is, or how you feel. Haven't we heard of the age-old saying: 'Sticks and stones may break my bones but words will never hurt me'?

So come on, let's bring back a society with Cojones, and preferably one with a good sense of humour.

Take Jeremy Corbyn, the former leader of Her Majesty's Opposition, the Labour Party. Not long ago he mouthed 'stupid woman' at Theresa May, the female UK prime minister. The public, and the media, were up in arms, saying his comment was sexist. Get a life. What utter nonsense.

Nobody dislikes Jeremy Corbyn more than me, but Theresa May *is* a woman. That's what she is biologically. If he thinks she's stupid that's his opinion. Who cares? When he denied it, when it was obvious to everyone what he said, that to my mind was worse. He blatantly lied. He should have stood up and had the Cojones to be honest and say, "Yes, I said stupid woman." Apart from that, no harm done. Let people show their distaste at his antics, and what he's done at the ballot box, but he can say what he likes really, particularly to himself!

Funnily enough, or should I say sadly enough, these days he's lucky he didn't get lambasted for using the word woman, such is the PC brigade's demand for 'gender neutrality', so as not to offend transgender people. The world has gone nuts.

I've already mentioned victimhood, and it seems to me society nowadays panders to the so-called 'victims'. In the last few years, our government has adopted policies largely known as austerity. Why? Because the country is in so much debt, we needed to start taking responsibility and stop spending money that we don't have. I remember what my mother said: "Neither a borrower nor a lender be." Wise words I would say. So we've had a government that decided we need to be more austere and tighten our belts. Seems perfectly rational to me.

If I get myself in debt, be that with the banks or credit cards, I have to take responsibility and pay my debts back. That's right. Pay back money that doesn't and never has belonged to me. And yet, all the victims have been up in arms about austerity. People complaining they're not getting the state handouts they used to get, people saying we should be borrowing more to give to them. I'll repeat, if I borrow money, I pay it back through my own work and industry, not by borrowing more and further deepening the debt.

And you know what, many of the people who complain about austerity are those who are too lazy to get a job, and have never taken responsibility for their own lives. Cojones is about character, and being a victor not a victim. It's about taking back control of oneself.

Many people now follow an extreme form of economic prejudice based on jealousy. Don't be jealous of the haves, do your best to **be** one of the haves instead by adopting the Cojones Code. Stop looking over your shoulder at others. By all means learn from them, but don't be jealous, it will get you nowhere, and I mean nowhere.

Here's another wise quote: 'You can't change the world, you can only change yourself.' How about having the Cojones to take the bull by the horns and take responsibility? That's more like it, and that's what this book is intended for.

All the victims want to do is blame others for not having the life they believe they should get, without 'going for it' themselves. Well Cojones is about ***doing, taking action*** and ***responsibility.***

Here's another one of my Cojones Ten Commandments laid out later: Be a Shepherd not a Sheep. Sadly, we live in a society of sheep.

Cojones is about regaining and having the strength to embrace a proper moral code. Who can you think of, whether you like them or not, who have expressed some of the gutsy traits we could all do with in our lives? (I will identify some of my own later in the chapter on Cojones Icons.) In actual fact, what role models or icons are there in today's society? Sadly, not many. But there are some.

Probably the most photographed person in the world is Kim Kardashian. For what? Doing a home sex video, that's what. Is that what people aspire to be? Or Katie Price, famous for her lowest of the low lifestyle, and for stripping off at any opportunity. Are these role models in any shape or form? Not to my eyes, nor anybody with a modicum of moral fibre.

We need more proper role models. Society needs more role models, and if people had the Cojones to be principled, to adopt much if not all of the Cojones Code, society may, just may, be a lot better.

There is always, of course, a balance.

I don't want to come across that I am angelic. I'm really not, but when my wife first came to live in the UK she was shocked that when I asked a waiter or waitress for a glass of water, I used to say "Sorry to trouble you." Some may say this is polite, and back then I would have agreed with you. But now? I question, what am I apologising for? Probably my existence!

And you know what else, in a similar way? If I felt I'd done something wrong to another, I used to apologise numerous times. Why? Possibly a reflection of my own lack of Cojones, or even basic self-esteem at the time.

Be polite – using a please, a thank you or a sorry costs nothing, but overdoing it is a sign of a lack of Cojones. This book will go some way to addressing that.

Social media

One of the biggest things in society now is social media. For sure, it's very clever and extremely useful if you know what you are doing. Personally, I'm a Philistine when it comes to social media.

But I look at Facebook, Twitter and Instagram and think we live in a world where connections are so limp, where people seek some sort of fake digital world for recognition and attention.

Take Facebook. I am on it, but I have never posted a picture or message about what restaurant I am dining at, or what I'm having for tea. What for? Why would people be interested in my cream cake or Danish pastry? I'm certainly not interested in theirs. I couldn't give a damn!

I mean, I know people who visit the Caribbean and spend their time posting pictures of themselves on Facebook. You've spent all that money going to one of the world's beauty spots, and you spend your time taking selfies on your smartphone so you can effectively tell people "Look at me, look at me." Pathetic. You're missing out on *being*, that's right, *being*, in such a beautiful place. How pathetic people really are today.

We live in a time where making these loose connections on Facebook (Facebook calls them 'Friends') is so easy, yet people are more lonely than they have ever been. I know people who post messages and pictures wishing their three-year-old child or their 100-year-old grandma a happy birthday. Why? We all know their three-year-old child or 100-year-old grandma isn't even on Facebook. They do it so that the sheep can feed their own needy attention-seeking diet, by saying, "Aah, happy birthday to little Mikey" or "Happy birthday to your 100-year-old grandma."

And do they really care? Of course not. Does the person putting up this message care about giving their three-year-old child or 100-year-old grandma a birthday message? No. It's about receiving the fake attention for themselves. Very sad. No wonder the majority of prescriptions written by doctors are for antidepressants.

Start looking to satisfy and make yourself happy by being real, which is what Cojones is about, and what this book espouses, rather than seeking fake and meaningless attention from those equally needy and sheepish people who most likely care little about you anyway.

So there you have it. I could write a whole book on this chapter alone, but I'm starting to rant a bit. OK, I'm starting to rant a lot, so will quit while ahead and just say that adopting the Cojones Code means you will be bringing an honesty, a transparency, an authenticity, a work code, a moral code, to a society that has desperately lost it.

You can't change the world, but if you adopt the Cojones Code and change yourself, you are doing your bit, I promise you that.

Read on and find out how.

CHAPTER 2:

MY STORY AND COJONES JOURNEY

You may find this chapter a tad self-indulgent and could, in theory, forward to the next chapter, but if you don't understand where I came from, in terms of my own journey, you'll possibly accuse me of not being real or of lacking the integrity with the messages I bring. By hearing about my own struggles you may see that the hardships make us and shape us for what comes next, and in this instance it's adopting a Cojones way of life – what I call the Cojones Code.

So, you may well ask, have you always been 'ballsy', bold and fearless? That's the question I used to ask when I used to see and hear all the successful people in the world, particularly the so-called self-help gurus. And the answer is a big NO. Of course I haven't, and of course I am not.

I'm not going to stand here, or sit (I am sitting) on my soapbox and convince you that I am perfection personified, and that being why you should listen to me. In fact, it's because I have been a frightened child (I still am at times), a person who has suffered severe self-doubt, low self-esteem and dragged myself out of it that I am in a better position to discuss what has worked for me, and in my experience for others as well.

I actually come from a family of super-talented worriers. Yes, brilliant, as they were and still are, so very good at it. It actually took me 40 years to realise what their worry was, and is. Even the worry they had for me. In fact, it took me 40 years plus to realise after learning from one of my many teachers, the leading psychoanalyst and astrologer Mavis Klein, that when someone says they are worried about you they aren't actually caring, they are actually being selfish and talking about and living according to their own fears.

So, I come from a family of worriers, people who see the fear and stumbling blocks in anything first, even if the positives far outweigh those possible negatives. I learned how to be negative through osmosis, worrying over many years about popularity, success, money, health and mortality. Particularly the latter two.

But the way you are, and I am no different, is a mixture of nurture and nature. My temperament from birth was a sensitive one in which being exposed to an atmosphere of negativity was the perfect environment for learning, and indeed adopting, that negativity and to go with it poor self-image.

And then, when I was seven, my dad went and got cancer didn't he – the bastard. Of course, it wasn't his fault, that's just the selfish me talking. He had bowel cancer and had his whole bowel removed, meaning at the age of 50, arguably his best years, he was effectively disabled of being in control of a vital natural bodily function, wearing a colostomy bag for the rest of his limited years. Pretty unpleasant for those witnessing it, not least a seven-year-old.

We were never told the extent of his illness, but that we could all see, and hear, as he was not even able to control the passing of wind at the dinner table. I can only imagine the mental torment he must have been going through, but I guess then I was of limited life experience and selfish, as we all are.

Talk about fear. He was naturally fearful of going out to friends, and we were fearful of our friends coming to us, in case they'd literally 'smell something' or certainly hear it, meaning we were all going to be embarrassed, notwithstanding the ridicule I was to receive in school.

My dad, a man a young boy was supposed to look up to as some sort of hero and pillar of strength, was reduced to a stricken man, and in some respects someone I was ashamed of. Cruel, I know, and of course today I realise what he must have been going through. Whatever self-esteem he did have must have popped the moment he came to after his major operation, and that damage certainly fed into me, not that I knew it at the time.

And it didn't end there. The misery of my dad's ill-health, that continued to worsen for the next seven years, led to my siblings who were older than me going out all the time to escape whilst I was at home to be my mum's pseudo 'replacement husband'.

I realised later on that at a time when a boy needs his dad to mould him into a young man, to instil manly courage, boldness and self-esteem, he was unable to do it, as he had been robbed of it himself. How could he? That job therefore was left to my mother, who was going through her own 'shit', worrying, yes worrying about my dad, nursing him, whilst raising us, particularly me, as I was the baby of the family.

I became rather miserable and unsettled as a kid at that time, and used to beat myself up about a number of things making me sad, and often so. One thing that gave me some light was at the age of 11, after having nagged and nagged and nagged my parents, I got my wish when we picked up a Golden Retriever puppy. I loved that dog, who we called Taffy (as he was from Wales), taking him for walks, obedience training, and clearing up his mess. Nothing gave me so much light as when my mum picked me up from school with Taffy. It still warms my soul just thinking about it.

But my dad got ill, and more ill, and with Taffy eating my green-fingered dad's beloved geraniums, the threats of 'getting rid of the dog' came regularly, and sure enough a few days after my Barmitzvah (a 13-year-old Jewish boy's coming of age), the man who catered for our party guests came and took our dog with my father's blessing, leaving me bereft.

This affected me so deeply that it took me 35 years to get another Golden Retriever, but eventually I did, as you will read later in the book.

After the death of my father when I was 14, I never realised for another almost 30 years the effect of environment and programming had on my psyche, my confidence and ability to enjoy life and be happy. My courage and belief in myself, let alone others, was not really there, and I never even realised it. I was lost, and drifted through school and university with no direction. My supposed fatherly guiding light was gone, and I was ill-equipped for many years to navigate through adulthood myself.

As I said, we are a combination of nature and nurture, but my nature is sensitive and wasn't tough enough at that time to go it alone in the world. The crazy thing is, I was always a 'good boy'. I never smoked, drank, took drugs or anything. Mind you, I never went out as a normal teenager as I felt compelled to stay at home and be with mummy!

But whilst I did suffer from fearfulness, lack of self-esteem, courage etc, I still got a degree, and seemed to get by and do stuff. I had obvious ability, although I never actually realised or recognised it.

When I got an honours degree in Estate Management, I walked out of the university after having got the result, thinking 'how the bloody hell did I manage that?' I never studied as diligently as I could or should have, nor had my heart in what I was studying, but still got a half-decent vocational degree, yet I gave myself no credit at all, putting it all down to sheer fluke.

Still I continued to drift, eventually getting a job as an assistant surveyor, which I hated. After having attended a conference for chartered surveyors, I thought to myself 'I could do this, and make a killing', so I left my job and set up a conference organising business.

It did OK, and that was my first real venture into the world of being ballsy. I had no experience in conferences, yet got the speakers, set the programme, organised the marketing material, booked a venue, did the letters and mailshots, as well as some phone selling, and arranged my first professional conference. However, I didn't make the killing I stupidly believed I would. I did break even, which sounds all right, but it was a low-budget affair, so I only put on one more, with 200 or so people attending.

I should have carried on and built a successful business, but immaturity got the better of me, as did fear – fear of worrying about attendees, and stupidly my short-sighted belief that I should be making that killing. No one was there to convince and calm me, Rome wasn't built in a day, so I gave up, extremely prematurely.

I then drifted more, before I eventually got a telephone sales job, selling conference spaces, and then advertising space. I failed at first, yet my boss kept faith in me and I eventually became the best in the company. He subsequently told me he always knew I could do it. I was still doubting myself of course, and hated the insecurity of worrying, yes worrying, where my next sale would come from. I left to go back to surveying, yet feeling perennially unhappy at not being able to find myself and do something that allowed me to express who I was, and my talents.

That's the bizarre thing: underneath all the self-doubt, miserableness, there was a multi-talented guy who actually rarely did badly at anything. As a young guy, I had unearthed talents that I took for granted. When I was at junior school I was quite a talented impersonator, often performing on stage. At 18 I found out I was a good singer and performed regularly. I'd taken up the guitar, and at 21 became a black belt in Tae Kwon-Do. I still thought I was a failure. That's a paradox in itself. Here I was, pretty good at martial arts, yet I kept getting beaten up, by myself.

Actually, I did use some of those talents somewhat. Singing became my opportunity to be noticed by people, particularly girls, although again I was painfully fearful of rejection. In fact, I expected it.

The bizarre thing is, I have always through the dark cloud that I always kept close to me done stuff. I may not have given myself credit for any of it, and certainly got no credit from my family, but I kept doing stuff.

Here's a classic story about my own Cojones when I started singing.

Me and my mates used to go every Monday to a famous pub called the Old Bull and Bush in Hampstead as they had a singer and acoustic guitar player performing covers. He used to ask if anyone had any requests, occasionally inviting people up to sing with him. One week I told my mates, "I'll get up there next week," to which their response was a doubting and mocking, "Yeah right!"

The following week the guy asked if there were any requests, to which I shouted out, "Return to Sender," to which he responded, "Do you want to come up and sing it?" I reluctantly but knowingly agreed, as I had decided that I was going to that previous week. And what happened? I brought the house down, people loved it. My mates were totally surprised at how good I was.

Despite my doubt, I also knew underneath that I had something. My demand of myself to prove to myself that I could do it was always there, and remains today. Perhaps the side of me that just 'knows' nervously punches the self-doubt side of me on the nose, but that is a major side of adopting Cojones. It's challenging those fears, those nerves, and I realise it has been something that has saved me, and I have done the same thing in other ways and other aspects of life.

I believe that this form of Cojones, that something underneath the self-doubt and negativity, is something that most of us have, and is what I call the Cojones fuel, enables us to do great things. Of course, the word great is subjective, but if *you* think it's great, then that's all that matters.

Don't get me wrong, the doubt, the aimlessness and feeling I wasn't going anywhere continued, but there have been some small fires burning inside of me forever, and in recent years the shadows have been more actively removed. Over a number of years, I have done numerous things that are a little bit way out. All the above: singing and playing guitar at gigs, doing impersonations at boxing dinners, and telephone wind-ups.

When I was in telesales, I used to entertain the lads in the office upstairs. I actually wound up Sir Alex Ferguson, the Manchester United manager, over the phone whilst he was in his hotel room in Barcelona, a few hours before he led his team to the European Champions League final against Bayern Munich.

True story. The boys upstairs found out which hotel the Manchester United team were staying in, so asked me if I would pretend to be Bobby Robson, the former England manager (as I said, I used to be quite good at impersonations). So I got on the phone, with loudspeaker on, the boys huddled round, and I got through to his hotel room. I chatted to him for about ten minutes as the late Bobby Robson. The boys were in hysterics.

Years later, when Sir Bobby passed away, a friend of mine called me to say he'd just heard Sir Alex eulogising on Sky Sports News, saying, "I remember he called me a few hours before the game against Bayern Munich to wish me luck." It was me, and I don't know if he knows that until this day.

I've also been a political analyst. This book is non-political but I used to debate Middle Eastern politics with high-profile politicians such as Ken Livingstone and David Miliband, on live radio. The usual doubters, when they heard I was to go into the lions' den against seasoned politicians, warned me against it. And yes, their warnings fuelled my self-doubt and fears, but yet again, something underneath all that forced me into that lions' den, and I came out on top.

It's interesting the number of people who claim to be your friend but instead try to put you off, or down, due to their lack of belief in their own ability. I didn't need them to give me self-doubt, as it was there already, but it did make it worse; but I always proved my doubters and myself wrong, and there's no greater feeling.

Only this year, as a political candidate, which I did for the experience of it, I was invited to be on BBC Radio on the Jeremy Vine show. My cousin, when he found out, said, "Be careful, that Jeremy Vine is very clever." Not once did he tell me that I was too. Only this time, all I took from his words was 'be prepared' rather than the old 'maybe I can't do it'.

I don't know if you're interested in my story as I am not an A-list celebrity, as that's what the average person is interested in. Not that I'd want to be. And anyway, what a stupid tabloid-driven term. What makes them A-list? Most of them are either actors who spend their lives not being themselves, or even talentless reality celebrities. So in reality, I think I offer something more real.

I'm like most people, everyday guy who's experienced some highs and lows, learned from them somewhat, but has hit upon a genuine epiphany that is real, cuts away the bullshit and delusion, encourages being authentic and real, and gets people from A to B in different areas of life. That's why I think you can do a lot worse than to learn from my lightbulb-based theories and learnings based on my own talents, experience, study, and to date, life story.

So, I've always had something innate that was a bit different, doing ballsy stuff. Singing, impersonating, performing, demonstrating, debating, selling, public speaking, pranking. After all of those and often not thinking twice about doing it, as well as people saying, "You've got a lot of balls," I realised that to do anything in life takes basic self-esteem and confidence, but to be successful, to be different and strive takes balls, hence the birth of Cojones.

We all need role models, and later on in the chapters on Cojones Icons I've highlighted some whose experience and success we can learn from and model to help us in our own quest for success.

To add to that, I've been very lucky, as I have met some inspirational people on my own journey. In fact, I have been lucky enough to have a great mentor, as well as friend, in Gary Leboff, who I mentioned in the Acknowledgements earlier. One of the top sports and performance coaches in the UK.

This is something I have also been fortunate in – that I am very intuitive and have consciously and probably subconsciously been able to realise who will be a positive influence on me. Gary, who I still see from time to time, has been a massive catalyst in the unearthing of Cojones. If you can, always seek out those who want the best for you selflessly, nurturingly, and honestly. I wouldn't be writing this today without him, as he pushed me to realise and recognise that Cojones is an idea and quality that I stick up for, and that I am indeed a reflection of Cojones and the brand.

If possible, you want to be your own positive mentor, but having somebody who is a positive influence in your life, and who can rationally and without emotion see things that maybe you can, but don't, or refuse to, can have a huge effect on your progress. I am lucky in this regard.

So in short, this is my story and the lead-up to the birth of Cojones.

I did mention, however, that I have always been, as a person, an eccentric, and strived to some extent to be different and do things differently. So in the next chapter I thought I'd share a few of my own Cojones moments, where I have been bold, audacious and achieved things in a somewhat obtuse way to get a result.

CHAPTER 3:

A FEW PERSONAL COJONES STORIES

I think that if life itself is to be lived to any sort of quality it does require some self-esteem. Although, I think self-esteem may be the wrong word, as many successful people have very low self-esteem. That said, I do think that adopting the Cojones mentality will go about boosting your self-esteem enormously, as you will discover when you put these ideas into practice.

I know you may judge someone's success by the wealth they have accumulated, or by the fame or status they may have. Success of any kind, though, is so subjective that I am simply going to come up with a few personal stories that help illustrate how I have put Cojones to good use in my own life.

I have been fortunate enough to have a fair amount of material success. I've been self-employed my whole life, and during that time have built up my own property portfolio, which took some balls, but I'm just going to hit on some stories that are more fun and interesting than the stereotypical 'I built a company from nothing and sold out for millions' ones. Not that I knock those or the people behind them in any way.

An Evening with a Hero

The first story I'd like to relate to you is a recent event I organised, with one of my heroes, the legendary Arsenal Football Club manager Arsène Wenger.

If you are from the UK you'll know who he is, as football (or soccer for my American readers) is simply the biggest sport in the UK and the world, and this guy was a hugely successful manager of one of the biggest teams for a record length of time – 22 years.

I had wanted to interview Arsène Wenger for a long, long time. Not only did he bring great success to a team I had supported since childhood, he also changed the face of English football with his ideas and methods. Nicknamed 'The Professor' due to his enormous intellect – he holds two degrees, speaks five languages fluently, and has a deep and profound mind.

As you can imagine, arranging an interview with him was going to be no mean feat. I had his phone number for some while, but despite me trying on numerous occasions, he never answered and for a few years I thought it was never going to happen.

He is a man in huge demand, even more so arguably after leaving his managerial position at Arsenal, but when he left I decided to hone in on him. Eventually I got hold of him, which was somewhat surreal after having failed for so long, and pitched him on doing a *Cojones Icons* interview. He was very polite and decent, in line with his reputation for being so, but politely declined. What a gutter!!

He did, however, give me an insight, which in turn gave me my lightbulb moment. He told me he did a lot of charity events. I've done a number of events and talks for charity, so subsequently and in due course managed to get hold of him again to see if he would be willing to do an event for a child bereavement charity I was closely connected with.

Now, why is this a Cojones story? Because when you hear the saying 'If you don't succeed, try, try again' I had to change it to 'If you don't succeed, try, try, try, try, try, try, try, try again and again and again'.

This man is virtually impossible to get hold of, and even harder to pin down. When he said to me, "Maybe I can do December" I was immediately on his case, for three months before finally getting him to confirm the date. And that was having already had to book a venue in the meantime!

A very busy man, and also someone who rarely does events of this particular format. Only when I received a text on the morning of the actual event could my mind be at rest that he was definitely going to show up, and that was after selling all tickets in a mere 72 hours. As it turned out, he did come, true to his word, which he is revered for sticking to, such is the character of the man.

In fact, it was a great event, raising thousands for charity, and interviewing him on a one to one only made me like and respect him even more, such was the interest I had in his answers. A true gentleman, and the moral of the story was that whilst I perhaps was overpersistent, to which I was deeply apologetic, my boldness, audacity and intent in pulling it off was evident, with even

Mr Wenger telling me on stage, "I think you did very well!" Praise indeed, and yes, Cojones.

Now, read on to learn how you can embrace Cojones, be more ballsy, in the quest for your own results and progress.

Sales, But Not as We Know It

As I mentioned earlier, I also had a stint in the hardest form of sales, as a telesales rep. I used to sell advertising space to banks around the world over the phone for $10,000 a page – cold calling.

Without wanting to blow my own trumpet, I became pretty good at it, and did a lot of business.

Naturally, I was rejected numerous times of course, as is the nature of the 'game', and as my boss Trevor used to say, sales is a combination of craft and graft. However, I also knew not to take a no very easily, exhausting all possibilities to secure a deal.

One hilarious deal came from a bank in Cyprus. I phoned them and pitched the decision maker (always pitch the decision maker), and ended the call saying I would call back in a couple of days.

When I tried to speak to the chap again, he never took my call, obviously deciding he wasn't interested.

My Cojones, out-of-the-box thinking went into overdrive. Knowing that people often feel more comfortable and have a natural rapport with their 'own', I called him posing as a Greek Cypriot calling myself George Polycarpou. I got the name as someone I was at university with was from Cyprus and had that name.

I can do voices, so I put on my best Cypriot voice, and immediately got put through to the boss, the decision maker, and the man I'd spoken to some days previously. All of a sudden his interest perked up, after me telling him I was from a Greek Cypriot background but London based, such is the patriotism of Greeks.

I ended up getting the deal!!

Most other salespeople would have given up the ghost. But I used audacity, chutzpah as well as my skill for doing voices to bring home the bacon so to speak, entertaining the office at the same time. A Cojones moment indeed.

There were other stories like this as well in that office. I did a similar thing pitching a number of banks in Egypt. The phone lines were poor in those days, and when I said my name was Keith Fraser they thought my name was the Arabic name Al Faisal. So sure enough, when I called them up I put on my best Arabic voice and called myself Al Faisal.

I won a lot of business with Arab banks being the aforementioned Al Faisal. Hilarious, and true.

Dating Apps – Who needs 'em!!

In the previous chapter you will have discovered my take on why the world needs Cojones, and badly, and none more so than in the world of social skills.

People, as I mentioned, seem to have replaced good old-fashioned human interaction with a smartphone. These days they get their kicks from a 'thumbs up' from a keyboard, or fake flannel about how amazing they look from people just as bored as they are by resorting to modern-day laziness – the smartphone.

People are replacing real human and natural connection with the fake virtual world and using a phone or computer to meet others.

And yet, you can go to the shops, to an event, a party, and meet people there, like most people used to, but many are afraid to now, as they hide behind the protective curtain of an app or website.

You want to meet your lifelong partner, then how about 'growing a pair' and getting out there into the world and meeting people – real people. I did that in a typically unconventional and Cojones way in meeting my future wife.

I was abroad in the Middle Eastern country of Israel in my rental car, when at the traffic lights an attractive girl pulled up next to me in the adjacent lane. I hooted, wound down the window and asked her for directions. And before you ask whether she was 'on the game' – no, of course not, you cheeky bugger!

The lights kept changing and at each lights she continued directing me. Then, out of the blue I cheekily said, "Look, I'm an English guy here on holiday who could do with being shown around, what's your number?" To my surprise, she started to tell it to me, and continued as the lights changed. Me having a good memory for numbers (not telephone numbers, I haven't had that much practice I can assure you), remembered it until I had stopped and put it into my mobile phone contacts list.

When I called her she said, "I must tell you, I have a boyfriend," and declined my invitation to get together. Me being the honourable guy thought if she does have a boyfriend I am not one to attempt to step on anyone's toes, and if she just had second thoughts, then I wasn't interested anyway, so left it there.

Five months later, I happened to be back in the country and found myself at a loose end one evening. What was I to do? So I scrolled down my mobile phone address book, and there was the girl I'd met at the traffic lights, right at the top (her name did begin with

A). I called her there and then. She remembered me, and as luck would have it, had recently finished with her boyfriend and we went out that night.

After that an overseas romance ensued, one thing led to another, she moved to England, and we're now just about to celebrate our 11th wedding anniversary!

You see what a bit of audacity and boldness can do? Who needs dating apps?! Opportunities are everywhere. You just have to look around for them and take the ACTION!

The Last Minute Valentine's Dinner Booking

Continuing on from the last story, one Valentine's Day I had forgotten to book a table for dinner.

You know what it's like on one of the busiest days of the year. If you haven't booked well in advance for that special place, you'll certainly be unlikely to get one at the very last minute, on the actual day.

Well, you would think so. If, however, you have audacity, cheek and Cojones, then your chances will certainly go up a notch. Here was a situation that you had the so-called most romantic day of the year but the possibility of no romance! Drastic times called for drastic measures.

I had tried to get a table at a nice place but had no luck. I therefore, as someone who was good at impersonations, decided to call a restaurant posing as a famous person. Amazingly, the first restaurant I called was delighted to accommodate me (or that famous person at least), and reserved me a great table to boot.

When we got there I apologised, and said I was the agent of the celebrity I'd posed as on the phone, and the person's wife came down sick at the last minute and sent me in his place. Lovely evening it was in the end too.

Cheeky, bold, audacious, even a tad underhand (for that I apologise, and don't condone), but shows you what a bit of thinking on your feet and Cojones can do, eh?!

Business Can Be Done Anywhere – Even Doing Your Business!

What does that mean you ask?

It's simply another off the cuff and off the wall story of mine that again highlights that opportunities are everywhere.

I was having a meeting in a business club in central London and had to answer a call of nature. Of course, when that call comes in I try not to delay. When I was at the urinal there was a chap next to me, but with his mobile phone to his ear talking, whilst 'doing his business' so to speak.

When he ended his call I cheekily said to the chap, "Business must be good!" He laughed, seeing the funny side, and we struck up a conversation, then and there in the men's room, telling each other what we do etc.

It turned out he needed a speaker/trainer for his sales staff at his IT firm, I said I'd call him and discuss some options in greater detail. After our telephone chat, he proceeded to book me to take some sessions with his staff, and of course paid me well for my services.

It just goes to show you again what can transpire when you have Cojones.

I can tell you, I have many more stories like this, but thought I'd give you a few just to give you an idea why I feel qualified to show others how to adopt a Cojones mindset.

CHAPTER 4:

THE SELF-HELP WORLD – ITS FALSE PROMISES AND LESSONS LEARNED

Did you pick this up thinking you were going to get another self-help book?

Did you buy it to feed your addiction to the infinite number of personal development books out there?

Have you already read loads of these type of books and thought to yourself I'll just buy one more, as it looks like *the* one that'll really make that difference in my life?

Or, are you looking for yet another self-help guru to tell you that you can do anything you want, are a reflection of the divine, are perfect in every way etc?

If the answer is yes to any of the above, then I want you to do me a favour: go and get your money back as this book isn't for you. You'd be wasting your time and mine. Let me tell you, most self-help books are a complete waste of time, re-hash the same crap, and help lost people become even more lost and actually encourage them to become delusional.

Why is it we live in a world where we have huge increases in fad religions such as Scientology or Kabbalah? Why is it that $550,000,000 a year in the US alone is spent on self-help books? Prescriptions for antidepressants, suicide rates, use of therapists, or even the number of therapists, coaches etc is at an all-time high, and growing.

Yet, surprisingly, as human beings we have never ever had it so good. In the West, and in the main, few of us here have experienced wartime, food rationing, lack of modern luxuries. We have connection to the world via the internet and social media, and yet people are still lonely and miserable and feel a lack of whatever. In a way, it doesn't make sense.

I wonder out of all the people who've read just one self-help book whether they found the difference they were looking for after reading it.

Of course not! 99% of it is utopian nonsense. We probably know it is, but we are so lost and desperate for the panacea that we think maybe, just maybe, this or that book will have the key that will unlock everything we've been searching for. Sorry everyone, time to wake up and smell the Colombian roast.

I certainly believe all of us have something unique and something to offer the world, and by employing some steps, often outlined in these books, we can get closer to realising that. But what tends to happen is that most people get a little emotionally aroused for a day or two if they're lucky, and that really is it. Then back to their normal life and rut.

I have a close friend who told me she was reading the well-known book *The Secret* because she had "a friend who read it and as a result of doing so got a Mercedes." She honestly believed that baloney, I kid you not.

It's great for Rhonda Byrne, the author, as it makes her a bit richer, probably a lot richer, as there are loads of people who like my friend fall for it like suckers, and then after a few days they find some other self-help book that they think will sort them out, and change their life forever.

Yes, the self-help economy is alive and healthy, as there are more and more people taken in by this bullshit. Excuse my French, or pardon monsieur ou madame!

I know this only too well, as I was one of them. I used to waste time on Amazon scouring the titles on offer to see which one was going to be **the one** that was going to click for me. Of course, that **one** never came.

Before I started the self-help book addiction, I decided I was going to go on a Tony Robbins weekend, as I thought that attending one of those was going to be the making of me. Although in truth, the two grand it was going to cost was probably going to be the breaking of me!

I was about to sign up when one afternoon I bumped into an old acquaintance in a coffee shop who saw me reading the book by the aforementioned Mr Robbins called *Awaken the Giant Within* and told me he attended a similar course that was cheaper and more local, called Outlook. I signed up instantly. It was very refreshing and made me feel great... for a few days, maybe a week, I can't quite remember. After that of course I went back to the old Keith, like everyone else, who eventually goes back to their old self.

Funny, I was so positively elated at the end of Outlook that when they announced places for the next level course, called Essence, and only a few places remained, I, like others, literally bit their hand off to sign up. This was great I thought, I am going to be a changed man overnight. Essence was equally great, and I thought I was already a changed man. Well, I was for a day.

The bizarre thing was that there was a feeling of sharing on these courses, a feeling of camaraderie, as I realised others were the same fragile human being like me, and to be fair that brought some healing to me.

Of course though, that wasn't enough. I then signed up for the week-long highest level course called Summit. This was the most bizarre. It was a week away in Wales where talking was prohibited, watches and mobile phones were handed in, and only basic belongings were allowed, with only basic food provided.

It was here that I realised that these self-help courses were not doing exactly what they said on the tin.

Every day, everyone had three minutes to do some 'sharing', on anything personal, or anything you were experiencing during the course. For me this was always a struggle, as I found it difficult to let go. After each 'sharing' session, we received feedback from other attendees and supervisors. One session, after I had 'shared', one of the supervisors told me he didn't see any changes in me, and said that Summit was the last course in the series, and that afterwards there would be nowhere for me to go.

They basically told me I was beyond help. How utterly irresponsible, or even negligent. Quite a hurtful thing to hear if you are somewhat lost and looking for inspiration, and all you hear is that this could be the end of the road, and that I am beyond help.

A few years after that, it dawned on me that none of these people were professionally or psychologically trained, and were mostly a bunch of quacks selling a course of delusion to 'lost' people.

I also noticed that the so-called graduates of these courses, who got sucked into the whole genre and became supervisors, were some of the most lost people I'd ever met, and only got more and more involved in the whole thing because they were, indeed, so bloody lost, and not the 'new people' they'd been told and sold that they would be. It was utterly laughable. People used to literally make these courses their life as regular supervisors. Why? Because they had nothing else in their life, that's why, and this gave them a place to be lost.

I'm glad I didn't spend in excess of two grand to attend Tony Robbins' 'yee haw, you are amazing' weekend. That doesn't mean I don't admire Tony Robbins. I do. But mostly as a salesman. He and other notable self-help gurus to my mind are brilliant salespeople, promoters, networkers, speakers, entertainers, but are they able to change people's lives and be the panacea they or others purport them to be? I very much doubt it.

Firstly, for me it was a journey. Or I should say, it **is** a journey. From self-help junkie to therapy junkie towards my own lightbulb moments. I realised I had something that was far more real. All the lecturing from gurus, be that in person or in books, was simply compacting all the non-stop thought and inner chatter. All that was actually needed in the end was that you **do**, without so much thought, that's actually all you need for change, results, and then success. And success may be simply having the insights, once clarity away from thought occurs. Because success isn't something you can measure, and shouldn't be measured by material wealth.

I know from my own childhood that you read about earlier that as long as you have your health, you have everything. But I guess we all take that for granted, and see that fact as a bit of a cliché. However, if you have your health, then actually you have what you need to go forth and evolve.

I would say go forth and multiply, but that sounds a bit biblical. But, when you think about it, if God really did say to Moses to go forth and multiply, I wonder if he genuinely meant procreate – even in our sex mad society.

To me what is never going to stop is evolution. The world's growth and change, hopefully for the better. So I think the whole meaning of 'go forth and multiply' means grow, evolve, and make things better.

And if it was the creator, or the divine, who said that and meant as I have interpreted it, then surely, by being self-critical, outwardly critical, negative, fearful, self-limiting, and all the other things that prevent us doing stuff, we are effectively going against God's word.

Or, put differently, if you don't believe in the man with a white beard, then by taking part in any kind of prevention of evolution and growth, we are simply going against what nature has given us, which is actually the ability to evolve and grow.

Look at the world now compared to 50 years ago, with technology, science, medicine. The world has evolved, because that is built into us, or is God's will if you believe in that. Personally, I believe God is, indeed, within us, and we do have, by command, the notion of 'go forth and multiply' literally inside each of us.

So, I really don't need some self-help guru, who is as perfect or imperfect as the rest of us, spouting his convoluted delusion to realise that we can achieve. All it takes is the realisation that you do have something underneath all the shit, and then rather than just dreaming about it, actually doing it, which means having the balls to do something. Yes, embracing Cojones.

I am sure I will come under fire for my words about this industry, and frankly I don't really care. As you will see later on in this book, I don't subscribe to the politically correct for fear of offence. As far as I see it, I like to say it as I see it. In fact, what further alarms me is that due to the explosion of the self-help field, there are infinite numbers of coaches and gurus who have no understanding of the human mind, who take a course lasting only a few days, and then go out and market themselves as a life coach.

Believe me, I know. When I was in that mindset I also did some coaching courses lasting just a few days, including some NLP (Neuro-Linguistic Programming) courses, and it was unbelievable the number of attendees who were already life coaches. NLP by the way is great, although again, numerous people do a few days' course in it and then believe they are fully equipped to tackle people's phobias. Pretty dangerous that, to my mind.

You will see in later chapters that your happiness and ability to achieve does not result from anything these quacks tell you. It comes from self-realisations, and most importantly, taking action! It really is as simple as that.

Again, don't get me wrong, there are some positive and powerful messages to be learned from reading some of these books, mostly the same message again and again and again and again, so if after having read a load you haven't gone any further despite the 'woody woodpecker effect' of the core message, then that should be further proof that the message alone isn't enough.

So if you really want to 'go forth and multiply' (at least in my interpretation of the phrase) then give up thinking that just by visualising yourself being the next Mark Zuckerberg or Barack Obama you will end up being so. Give up believing that what you think about will come about. When I was a teenager I used to think about the film star Michelle Pfeiffer, but it never came about, I can tell you.

I liken the self-help purveyors to the nouveau politically far left wing that has now gained popularity here in the UK. The utopian ideal that the world can all live in peace, where we are all best friends by giving in to everyone's demands and appeasing extremists, simply doesn't work in the real world.

We'd all love to live in the perfect world, but on a macro-level this does not exist, and will never exist. What can exist is living in your own perfect world, as only you can judge whether it's perfection. And if your world, your inner world I mean, isn't perfect, then you, and only you, really have the power to make it perfect.

There's a saying by the writer and philosopher Aldous Huxley: "I wanted to change the world. But I have found that the only thing one can be sure of changing is oneself." How true that is. And if people focused on only making themselves better, the world would be better without trying to change it.

The same goes for happiness, achievement, whatever that looks like. Ultimately, only you can make that a reality and embrace the boldness to take what lies beneath and use it for your own good or that of others. That's what Cojones is all about.

So there you have it. This book, the whole notion of Cojones, is matter of fact reality and not external delusion. It doesn't beat around the bush. I won't tell you anything because that's what you want to hear (that's for election campaigning politicians); I will tell you how it is, and if you choose to take it on board, then great.

If you don't take any of it on board of course, then actually that's your choice, or problem as it may be.

I know, I'm somewhat blunt. Actually, that's what the world needs these days in my eyes. A bit of honesty. And that's what I offer.

CHAPTER 5:

TRANSACTIONAL ANALYSIS (TA), COGNITIVE BEHAVIOURAL THERAPY (CBT) AND NEURO-LINGUISTIC PROGRAMMING (NLP)

Of course, I know what you're thinking and I know what you're going to say.

You've read the first few chapters and my take on the self-help world, and now I am dedicating a chapter to not one, not two, but three 'self-help' or psychological theories or practices.

My criticism though is not of the different psychological theories (as these are researched by experts in their fields), but of the promises made by the so-called gurus, or practitioners, because the large majority of them are not. Also, two of the three above titled theories are more psychological theories or practices/interventions with accepted and tested application.

There are, of course, literally, hundreds of types of therapy, all of which are very similar, but the three I have chosen are because I have some experience in them and also are among the most popular.

Transactional Analysis (TA)

This is a wonderful theory of human nature and psychological language, developed in the 1950s by the late Eric Berne and made famous by his book *Games People Play*. It is actually an extension of Freudian psychoanalysis in that our personalities are directly determined (often unconsciously) by our experiences in the first few years of our lives.

The foundation of TA being that none of us are just one person. In fact, we're not two, but three people, or ego states as they are known. That's right, each and every one of us is actually made up of three selves, known as Child, Adult and Parent ego states, and we switch from one to another at any time, for however long, throughout our lives. All three ego states are equally needed for effective functioning and healthy emotional being, but different situations are better dealt with by one ego state than the others, as ego states are basically divided into our thinking self, our believing self and our feeling self.

The second foundation of TA is that human beings share our lifelong need to be stroked or acknowledged in some way. That doesn't mean like a cat or dog is stroked, although it could be physical, but I mean largely emotionally.

Human beings need some form of acknowledgement, and a stroke could be a simple 'hello', a handshake, a pat on the back, a nod, a gift, or indeed any type of interaction. It is basically our psychological or emotional food, and we cannot live without it, which is why solitary confinement is such a real punishment for criminals.

Of course, like we need food to live and nourish us, we need strokes to do the same, albeit psychologically. And in the same way as food, we can eat junk food to satisfy our hunger and to survive (albeit badly if that's what our diet consists of), we can also survive on negative strokes. Negative strokes being an insult, a dirty look, a smack etc. According to the theory of TA, our complexities as human beings relate to the mixture of strokes, both the positive and negative ones we receive, and indeed to which particular ego state.

Our feeling self is our Child ego state, our thinking self is our Adult ego state, and our believing self is our Parent ego state.

What makes TA interesting to me is this concept of ego states, as we realise as mentioned that as human beings we are not one self but three, and we can make more sense of our life once we truly know this.

Interactions, thoughts and feelings of course, in the context of this book, why we do, or do not, or are able or not, to strive, take action, be bold and courageous are determined by the way each ego state is working, or not. This concept is highlighted by everyday judgment of something or someone, or the notion of making up one's mind, and the fight between your different beliefs, feelings and thoughts, desires and wishes, ie the debate between the different parts of yourself – your ego states.

As my old mentor Mavis Klein, from whom I learned much of this fascinating theory/language (check out some of her books on the subject) taught me: in simple terms our Parent usually acts like your parents do in judging what is right and wrong, our Adult is our rational self and acts like our computer, and our Child acts emotionally and expressively with feelings for good and bad.

Whilst everyone is made up of these components, most people have uneven levels of energy dedicated to any particular ego state, which is where part of the problem lies. Because if you have too little energy in your Adult ego state, then perhaps you don't rationalise matters enough, meaning you judge them from an emotional place. Or perhaps you have too much energy in your Adult ego state, and therefore your judgment or even personality lacks emotion, making you perhaps more robotic as a personality.

You may have too much energy in your Parent ego state, meaning you live by many shoulds, should nots, musts and must nots, which in relation to Cojones could prevent you moving forward as you are prevented from doing so by your blind loyalty to your Parent beliefs, which often require questioning by one of the other ego states (another part of you) in order to navigate effectively around them.

If you have too much energy in your Child ego state, you are likely to do things without any thought based on belief or rationale, meaning you do things too much on impulse, which can be good in adopting the Cojones mindset, but these types of people and their decisions can often be unreliable.

Whilst most people have an uneven level of energy in different ego states, which is possibly why we have the age-old saying 'different strokes for different folks' – and let's face it, the world would be pretty boring if everyone had equal balance in each – it is important to negotiate with that side of your personality (or ego state) to ensure correct decisions and the best outcome for any part of your life is arrived at.

Using techniques that we will look at in CBT and NLP (the linguistic side) will, I believe, ensure you do use the energy in the ego state you need, to embrace and adopt the Cojones Code. In my view, it would make sense that the most adept ego state, being bold, thinking outside the box, saying it as it is, for adopting Cojones is the Child ego state, but the others have to come into play in the debate to some extent so that the Child ego state's behaviour isn't totally unreliable.

I feel it necessary to discuss TA as I think it is the easiest psychological theory for understanding the makeup of human personality that I know of. By grasping that we are all more than one person, or ego state, and at any given moment too, how we behave and do different things at different times and contexts, then we can more consciously move into the appropriate ego state to achieve a particular goal or outcome.

Two approaches of doing so can be to use the basics of language, to yourself or maybe another, that I will highlight using the interventions of CBT and/or NLP to move yourself in that direction.

CBT or Cognitive Behavioural Therapy

As I referred to earlier, like most people I have had many episodes of low mood, low self-esteem, and particularly self-defeating thought, and after advice I went to see a trained psychologist in the practice of Cognitive Behavioural Therapy.

So what is it you may ask if you haven't heard of it? Probably you have. Of course, I am no expert in CBT, but the premise of the theory is very clear and indeed, on the face of it, makes a lot of sense. So based on my experience, and use of the proactive, here is my interpretation of it.

What gives us a strong clue is the main word in its title: Cognitive – ie involving cognition. Cognition being thought or perception. Cognitive Behavioural Therapy is based on the premise or idea that your thoughts and attitudes, and not external events, create your moods.

Have you ever had an argument with someone close, such as your parents or spouse, and as a result your whole world seems gloomy? You begin to think that your whole world is caving in, you can't cope, your business is going to go bankrupt, your partner will dump you, you're not good enough, and a whole raft of thoughts follow.

Of course, all those thoughts lead you to feel awful, sad, demotivated and possibly depressed. Those thoughts, although they appear real at the time, are the sole cause of the way you **feel,** and of course your actions, *or lack of them,* would follow. You see, the thoughts themselves are normally erroneous, but can be rationalised under CBT methods, supposedly making you feel better, and therefore more effective.

As David Burns, one of the most well-known practitioners, points out in his book *The Feeling Good Handbook,* under the CBT model you effectively, or supposedly "learn to change the way you think, the way you behave, and the way you feel."

CBT therapists are therefore of the mindset that the negative and erroneous thinking patterns that we employ cause us to feel sad, depressed and ineffective, and when you think about the issue at hand in a more rational and realistic way, you will experience greater self-esteem and of course productivity and success, which is what this book is largely about.

In terms of Cojones then, that would point to the fact that many of us, when we want to do something, based on this model depend wholly on the quality of our thoughts as to whether we will be more inclined to do the things that we need to, to obtain results. Often our erroneous thoughts lead us to stopping ourselves from being bold and audacious, and having Cojones.

I think the CBT model for pushing yourself forward in numerous situations can be very effective. In many scenarios I have had fear, but then once my rational inner voice has spoken and softened that fear, if not eradicated it completely, I can keep going towards my goal.

You will see, the whole subject of thought is taken to another level in the next chapter on the Three Principles, but I do believe the notion of self-defeating thought is partly at the heart of non-action and authenticity, so employing some CBT concepts is indeed useful to grow a pair, albeit not the be all and end all like any of these psychological theories.

Of course, the CBT model goes further, as it identifies the various types of erroneous thinking we all employ at some stage or another that result in the full range of negative feelings and subsequent behaviours, be it sadness, hopelessness, worry, panic and anxiety, guilt, shame, anger and more.

All the above feelings are connected in some way and intertwined, but the foundational connecting factor is **thought** of course, or I should say the incorrect or inappropriate use of it.

For the record therefore, let me list some of the faulty thinking patterns that lead to the feelings I have just outlined, and link them to Cojones – or *doing/being bold, audacious/thinking outside the box.*

1. *All or nothing thinking* – ie you see things in black or white with nothing in between. For example, if you do something that isn't absolutely perfect, you see it as total failure.

How it relates to Cojones? There is nothing wrong in striving for the best. In fact, in whatever you do there is nothing wrong in doing it to the best of your ability at any given moment, as you will always know that you've given your all at that particular time. But that feeling of 'If only I'd have done this, I could have got that' is awful, as it means you spend way too much energy on what I call post-mortems.

If you are only interested in perfection, or things going to perfection, then you are being wholly unrealistic, and if you see anything you do that is less than perfection as failure, more often than not you will think 'why bother?' meaning you don't do it at all.

The truth is, as you will see in my Cojones Ten Commandments, Cojones is about having a go. Throwing the dice. Perfection doesn't exist in any realm. Why not change the thinking to 'I'll do what I am able to or my utmost in that particular moment'? Then you will be more likely to get off first base.

2. *Generalising* – something happens to you, and automatically you believe it will *always* be like that, or everything is always like that.

How it relates to Cojones? There are numerous examples of all of these, but let's take a couple. You ask a girl for her telephone number and she rejects you, leading you to in the future never asking another girl, as you think you'll get rejected again.

Or, you made an offer to buy a property. It was accepted, only for you to be gazumped and the purchase falls through, resulting in you not looking at any other properties as you think **every** offer you make will eventually fall through. This is very limiting, and again prevents you doing something you would have liked to do, only because in your mind you think **all** future similar scenarios will result in the same disappointment.

3. *Discounting the positive* – effectively you fail to recognise any good in any situation, be that a job done, or the state of your life. Trust me, I'm an expert at this!

How it relates to Cojones? This is a classic, and as I just said, one I've been guilty of and am still guilty of, and I'm sure you have been too, at some point. Actually, I can tell you a story that only recently happened. I was driving with my mother past a guitar shop and saw in the window guitars for young kids. I told my mother I'd like to get one for my son who's four years old. Her response was, "Well he might hurt his fingers." I mean if we all thought like that, where would the Eric Claptons or Hendrixes of this world be? She failed to recognise the beauty of seeing a young boy learning an instrument.

When you discount the positive, you effectively disable yourself from striving, from growing. Well what would be the point with that kind of mindset?

By the way, my response was, "Why cross the road to that dress shop, as there's a chance you could be knocked over by a car?"

4. *Jumping to conclusions* (mostly negative) – for example, your long-term girlfriend or boyfriend has gone for a drink with a friend. You automatically think they've met up with someone else and cheating on you.

5. *Mind reading* – you, on default, believe you know what someone is thinking, or will think (often about you), and normally negative of course. By the way, the quote 'you wouldn't be bothered so much about what people think of you when you realise how seldom they do' helps in this case.

How it relates to Cojones? I can tell you that in planning my own *Cojones Icons* series on the Cojones TV YouTube channel, I knew I had to get high-profile, interesting guests to interview. When I contacted the subjects, people like Nigel Farage and Alastair Campbell, I could have thought 'they won't want to be interviewed by me, as who am I?'. Yes, I had those thoughts momentarily, but had the 'I don't know what they are thinking, and who cares, I have nothing to lose' thoughts. Yes, the rational thoughts that meant I had a bloody go.

Most people would have simply chickened out.

6. *Predicting the future* – the title says it all, and again, it normally means you predict things will turn out badly for you or whatever it is you are planning or want.

How it relates to Cojones? Similar to mind reading or jumping to conclusions, by predicting the negative future, you often don't do whatever it is you want to, or you do it badly, in some form of self-fulfilling prophecy, which means you will inevitably give up soon enough anyway. What a great shame.

7. *Magnification* – you overexaggerate the negatives, or your Achilles heel, and underestimate your qualities and skills.

How it relates to Cojones? Many successful people I have met are often limited in intelligence and talent compared to others, and don't actually see their limitations but go for it anyway, and often succeed. Yet often the most talented people overmagnify and see their own 'negatives' meaning they don't get off first base. How different it would be if we didn't magnify our own deficiencies.

8. *Negative emotional reasoning* – you believe the truth in your negative interpretation of things, ie you believe that your reasoning, and negative reasoning, is reality.

How it relates to Cojones? You will see in the next chapter in more detail how we believe our thoughts are our reality, so when one negatively interprets events, and our everyday lives, how is it possible to take the action necessary that will lead to a positive outcome? Very difficult, if not unlikely even.

I am a collector of quotes, with my favourites being listed at the end of this book, but as Henry Ford said: "Whether you think you can, or you think you can't – you're right." Well if you negatively interpret things, even if you do them, and you likely won't, you have a far greater chance of messing them up with this type of thinking.

9. *Should-ing* – you tell yourself and others that things, or yourself, or others, should be this way or another.

How it relates to Cojones? This type of behaviour, or language/ self-talk is also very limiting, and prevents you from going forward. I refer to it later when I look at NLP linguistic models, but again, shoulds are a form of rules that create stress, every single time.

We are always told that stress kills us, so 'shoulds' effectively kill us. Need I say more? Maybe not, but I will, as should-ing indicates a black or white way of living, judging things. If the likely outcome is likely to be somewhere in the grey, rather than the black or white that you believe in, aren't you demotivating yourself from the off? And even if you do do what it is you are trying, this form of stress will limit the quality of the outcome you seek anyway. Again, very limiting. And trust me, I know from personal experience. I am from a family of 'should-ers'!

So, as you can see, in terms of psychology it is understandable that when people adopt these erroneous debilitating thinking habits they give themselves all sorts of unhappy feelings, leading to an array of mental illnesses and personal restrictions as to what they think, say and do.

In terms of Cojones and growing a pair, if you employ any of the above thoughts, then you are possibly limiting yourself in terms of your ability to take the desired action at all, and if you do, then you will likely lower your chances of success as a result.

Does footballer Lionel Messi play half as well with a sprained ankle? Of course not. He will likely not play, or play well below his incredible ability. This is a pretty good analogy.

So, let's take a typical CBT homework chart to enable you to change the way you do things in the name of authenticity and results, and from inertia to action.

Next time you want to do something, anything, but stop yourself, see if you can identify the thought and self-talk that you are using. So here goes:

Firstly, what is the situation, ie where you are stopping yourself doing something? For example, I can't go for that audition as they will hate me as soon as they see me.

Automatic Thought	Distortion Type	More Rational Thinking
Maybe I'm not as good a singer as I thought	Discounting the positive	I've sung in public for years and always been well received. When I sing in my band, I get big applause most of the time, etc, etc
I'll sing out of tune	Predicting the Future	Why would I? How can I be so sure? I have been singing for years, and I've 99% of the time sung in tune.
I'm afraid of the unknown	Predicting the Future	Tomorrow is the unknown, so is the next day, and so is the next. When I cross the road, I could get knocked over by a car. Everything in the future is unknown, but doesn't stop me doing something, and I still do it.

So as you can see, and I am sure able to relate to, we are often our own worst enemy. Many of these irrational thoughts and self-talk messages are taken on in our minds from family and peers. So screw them, and even screw your own negative limiting self. Do you want to do stuff or not?

If you write your thoughts/self-talk down, and then attempt to be more rational, then you will start to say, "Fxxk it, I'm going to do this"!

Neuro-Linguistic Programming (NLP)

I'm not trying to blind you with all these psychological interventions, but by having a basic understanding of them, as well as one of our own selves, it allows us to move forward.

One reason I am anti much of the self-help guru stuff, particularly the books, is that people who read them believe that just the reading of them will do the trick in making them who or what they want to be. This is being off the beaten track to say the least.

One of my Cojones initiatives was my Cojones TV YouTube channel, which I used as a research tool for finding out what is between the ears of ballsy people. One of the interviews I did for the *Cojones Icons* series is with Alastair Campbell, the hugely successful spin doctor who was one of the architects of the British Labour Party's victory in three successive general elections.

One thing he said to me that speaks volumes here is that most people **want** to win, but the winners are the ones who have the **will** to win. Can you see the difference?

I mention this as for anyone to embrace the Cojones Code they have to have the *will* to do so, as opposed to simply *saying*, "I wish I could do that." If you want to, then that's not enough. If you have the will to, then you're on the way.

Neuro-Linguistic Programming, or NLP as it's called. What is it? There are actually numerous definitions, but let's simplify it and start by breaking down each individual word:

- Neuro: The brain/mind/body, and how it works.

- Linguistic: The language we use to describe our world and make sense of our experience.

- Programming: Sequences and patterns of thought and behaviour based on the above that help evaluate situations, solve problems and make decisions.

The founders of NLP studied successful people in order to analyse effective human behaviour, with focus on language of course, brain patterns, and how words and actions link together to form programmes or sequences of behaviour.

There are numerous books on this subject and I am fascinated by all of them, but I am only going to focus on what I consider relevant to Cojones, and about growing a pair, as that's what this is about.

So, what I am going to do is KISS. No, not physically, I am married, but as the acronym says, **K**eep **I**t **S**imple **S**tupid and refer to the part of NLP that I believe to be the most relevant, ie the linguistic side of the subject. This will enable you to communicate more effectively with yourself and others. Mostly yourself in this instance.

How you communicate with language is a key part of NLP. In conversation with yourself and others we unconsciously use three filters which transform what we experience through our senses (Visual, Auditory, Kinaesthetic) into language. These three filters are: deletion, distortion and generalisation, and they can work positively, or indeed negatively.

So, here we go:

Deletion: Being selective about certain experiences and deleting certain information from yours when you express yourself.

Distortion: Creating from others' words or actions a meaning that is not necessarily true or based on minimal evidence.

Generalisation: Believing something to be universally true based on your, or limited experience.

There are in fact many crossovers between the language identified in our filters and those we use when we spot erroneous thinking in the CBT model, and because of that we will bring the two together to ensure a Cojones behaviour and mindset in due course.

In a similar way, once we have identified the language filter, we can change the language or ask ourselves or others questions to gain greater understanding of the true experience, or indeed change our own thinking and therefore feeling and behaviour, and importantly, resultant action of course.

To be more specific, by asking certain questions under each filter we can:

- Deletion: gather more information

- Distortion: clarify a truer meaning

- Generalisation: identify a limitation, thus offering more choices

To better understand what we're saying here, take a sentence such as 'Man has walked on the moon'. Assuming the type of filters outlined above, what questions could you ask to obtain more understanding of the statement?

How about:

- Which man specifically?

- Or who specifically?

- Only one? or more than one man?

- When exactly?

- So what?

We humans have to use such language filters. When we delete information we are expressing what we think is most significant; when we distort, we express what has meaning for us; and when we generalise we express a consistency that we believe is relevant to our experience.

So let's start unpicking these with just a few statements you would perhaps use in the absence of Cojones – I have specified the title of each type but don't pay too much attention to these labels or titles.

DELETION

Deletion	Statement	Intervention
Simple Deletion	I feel scared	About what?
Simple Deletion	I don't know	What specifically don't you know?
Comparative Deletion	That is harder	Harder than what?
Nominalisations (Words that are Abstract)	I want to make a good impression	How specifically do you want to impress others?
Unspecified Verbs	They intimidate me	How specifically do they intimidate you?
Lack of Reference	People don't like me	Which people in particular?

DISTORTION

Distortion	Statement	Intervention
Complex Equivalence	With that personality he/ she must have lots of friends/ be very successful	How exactly does that personality mean that?
Cause & Effect	His telephone manner makes me intimidated	How does his manner make you feel intimidated?
Mind Reading	He's not going to like me	How do you know that?
Mind Reading	He'll be annoyed with me?	What lets you know that?
Lost Performative	It's hard to be successful	According to whom?

GENERALISATION

Generalisation	Statement	Intervention
Universal Quantifier	They never talk to me	Never??
Universal Quantifier	I'm always rejected	Always??
Modal Operator of Necessity	I mustn't/ can't call	What would happen if you did?
Modal Operator of Necessity	I have to follow a different path	What would happen if you didn't?
Modal Operator of Possibility	I can't speak to that girl	What would happen if you did?
Modal Operator of Possibility	There's no way I could do that	What would happen if you could?

Now please trust me when I say I don't want to blind you with science, but through my own experience I believe the above have great relevance in the subject of Cojones.

I can guarantee, whoever you are, that at numerous points in your life the language you use to others, and indeed others have used to you, and perhaps most importantly, the language you use to yourself, has involved many of these communication filters, and I would say in the grand scheme of Cojones, may well have impacted your courage, your boldness, your audacity, your ability to think outside the box, and therefore prevented you from the outcome and results you deep down would have liked or loved.

So, here's an exercise for you to do, but before we do it, here is a quote that will push and encourage you to do it:

"Twenty years from now you will be more disappointed by the things you didn't do than by the things you did." Mark Twain

I want you to think back over the course of your life. Do you remember the times you wish you did something but stopped yourself? That could be anything:

- It could be asking that girl on a date (apologies girls, I would say asking a boy but I am a traditionalist, sorry)

- It could be starting that business

- It could be going skiing

- It could be expressing yourself to someone

- It could be applying for that job

- It could be going for an audition

- It could be writing a book

It could be anything, but think back, just for now, at all or some of the things you *haven't* done.

I know, you will start to get that painful tinge of regret, but hey, you can use this pain to fuel your change to make amends in the future.

Write down just five examples now of the times you didn't do something, and next to it I want you to write down the language others used to communicate against your idea or the self-talk you used to stop yourself doing something:

WHAT I WANTED TO DO

What I Wanted to Do	Negative Talk from Others / Self
1.	
2.	
3.	
4.	
5.	

Well done. I know, you feel regretful, as you would. But that's the past, this is about learning from it. Now, using some of the interventions highlighted above, write them down in reference to each one.

You should, by doing this exercise, realise that with the right intervention you would possibly have acted differently, and in a task ahead instead actually *do it*.

And if you'd have failed after doing so, so what? Actually, according to NLP there is no such thing as failure, only feedback.

Putting it together

With all three subjects highlighted in this chapter – TA, CBT and NLP – they will enable you to understand yourself, your behaviour, communication and of course action. First of all, it is to my mind vital to know yourself better. All three give you help to do that. I know in NLP for instance, practitioners say what you did before, or the past, is irrelevant, as there are ways to ensure you act differently in the future. I wholly disagree.

If you were walking with a limp for example, it would certainly help to know why. Whether that be because you have a sprained ankle, or you have one leg shorter than the other, or even you are just plain drunk. By knowing which, you'd know what to remedy and therefore how to go forward, and that's why I believe all these three help you understand yourself and then enable you to make amends.

With CBT and the meta model within NLP particularly, you will be able to consciously make the changes that will enable you to grow a pair and do what you need to do. If you want to know your three selves better as part of the TA model, I recommend a number of books to allow you to explore this subject, particularly titles written by my own TA teacher, Mavis Klein. There are also books to assist you to delve deeper into CBT and NLP.

For now, whatever it is you *want* to do, try bringing to the conscious your thoughts and language, and then see how you can take the first step to being bolder, and yes, growing a pair.

CHAPTER 6:

THE THREE PRINCIPLES

I will be talking further about how we are all so full of contradictions, although that is pretty evident when you consider we are all effectively three people, as highlighted in the section on Transactional Analysis. And of course, and rightly so, you will note that I have, in the chapter dedicated to TA, CBT and NLP, dedicated considerable time to our thoughts.

Well, once you look at the Three Principles in some detail you'll notice some further contradiction but enlightenment.

So, what are the Three Principles?

Well, these were first articulated by Sydney Banks in the 1970s, a welder born in Scotland. According to Banks' verbal accounts, as recorded at lectures, he realised the Three Principles while attending a marriage seminar in British Columbia, Canada.

The seminar encouraged couples to *let their feelings out,* be honest, and argue with one another. Discouraged by the process, Banks and his wife prepared to leave the seminar. As they were doing so, Banks became engaged in conversation with a therapist also attending the seminar. Describing himself as *an insecure mess* at that time, Banks began elaborating on all the ways in which he felt insecure. The therapist's response, "*I've never heard such nonsense in all my life,*" was a revelation to Banks:

"What I heard was: there's no such thing as insecurity, it's only thought. All my insecurity was only my own thoughts! It was like a bomb going off in my head... It was so enlightening! It was unbelievable... [And after that] there was such beauty coming into my life."

I know, you're probably thinking 'stop the record, you sound like the rest of the self-help gurus you profess to dislike'. Actually, I keep telling you I don't dislike them, I just doubt a lot of them. But please bear with me.

According to Banks, as a result of his own lightbulb moment, he was able to articulate the Three Principles, explaining in its entirety human behaviour and feeling states, and how they are responsible for the creation of all human experience.

So what are they? Here we go:

Mind – The universal mind, the energy behind life. You may call it the divine, or God, but actually anything we see and more is the physical form of energy. We, as humans, are a mass of energy. A mass of trillions of cells made up of, yes you've guessed it, energy. Plants, flowers, rivers, the sea, animals, literally everything is made up of energy. The energy behind life itself. I'm no scientist by the way, so I'm just trying to simplify it.

Consciousness – Our awareness and our ability to have an experience.

Thought – The energy behind the experience. The creative force behind our own life, and our ability to guide our way through it.

The Three Principles is an understanding, not a therapy nor intervention, it is an explanation of what is, and practitioners will tell you that by merely recognising on a deep level this understanding, you come to realise that your whole experience of life is derived from the 'inside out' and not, as most of us believe from the 'outside in'. So if all your experiences, yes I mean all, are derived from your thoughts, then actually nothing that you experience can be blamed on anything outside of yourself because the experience is wholly created by your own perception.

Emotions therefore are borne solely from your thoughts, and when we deeply know and understand that their power dissipates, ie when we stop thinking them, their power simply dies. Our emotions appear real, but when viewed from a different angle they become no more than an illusion.

To make it simpler, I read a wonderful anecdote of this in a book titled *The Relationship Handbook* by a well-known Three Principles purveyor, George Pranksy:

You are in the ticket queue of a cinema, suddenly a large man pushes in front of you without a care that you've been patiently waiting for the last 20 minutes. No apology and no consideration for you at all. You're naturally enraged and about to confront this inconsiderate bastard, but just as you are about to, you see he's carrying a white stick and wearing dark glasses. From feeling angry, you now feel awful for being so judgmental and annoyed. Naturally you now keep quiet, and don't feel aggrieved with this man any more. The man behind you sees this and you tell him about your error.

The man behind you laughs out loud and says he knows this man, and that actually the 'blind man' is nothing of the sort, and just a trickster, and uses this ploy to jump long queues. All of a sudden, you're angry again. More angry in fact. Fuming! Your blood is boiling. You actually want to physically eject this chancer. How could anyone possibly disrespect the blind and be that low?

At that moment, you're just about to take a swing when some other fella tells you the man behind you is actually the trickster, and the guy in front of you is, indeed, blind!

You're utterly vexed now. A rollercoaster of emotions (thought derived of course) now – sheer confusion actually. But at that moment you see a man with a microphone and with him a cameraman, telling you you've been the subject of a prank organised by a friend of yours for *Candid Camera*. (If you are too young to remember this programme, it was a TV programme that literally played pranks on people.)

Can you see the relevance of this story? It shows that surely via your thoughts at a particular moment, in a particular context, your emotion was different – from anger, to guilt, to anger, to possibly humour. As the interpretation of the situation changed, and yes, you've got it, your thoughts, so did your emotions, and your feelings.

Now, in the same way, let's say as an example you'd love to join in a radio debate (or anything that makes you literally fill with nerves). You ring up, and get put on hold with the programme in the background as you're about to go live on air. You consider putting down the phone as you're so nervous. Then, at that moment the doorbell rings, you put the phone down (as you have to in order to answer the door), and it's your favourite aunt who's brought over your favourite homemade shepherd's pie for you. Your nerves are gone. Just like that! As legendary British comedian Tommy Cooper would have said.

So change of context and change of thought means change of emotion.

I know you avoided doing something nerve wracking, which is the opposite of Cojones which should mean stepping up to the plate, but what it shows is how easy your feelings change, and once you see that, do you really need to take your thoughts seriously, or your emotions? Not really. Although easier said than done, as our thoughts and perceptions do seem real in that moment. But your thoughts, which lead to your emotions, only appear real at the time, and considering you can see now how quickly that can change, they are nothing more than a mirage.

Think about it in another different way. Ever had a bad dream? Stupid question. We all have. How real does that dream seem when you are having it? Totally real, right? Sometimes horribly real. And when you wake up you may still *feel* the 'fag end' of the emotion, our physiological reaction, but since you have realised it is only a dream, yes, thoughts you had when you were asleep, they no longer have the power over you as you know they aren't real.

So, once you can understand that your thoughts only *appear* real, like your dreams, but aren't, you will be empowered to do so much more, which includes growing a pair, following the Cojones Code.

Now, looking at this further, let me ask you this. If you're nervous and breathing fast, what do you do? OK, OK, I know you can take deep breaths to consciously help you take in more oxygen, but what happens if you do nothing? That's right, your breathing will eventually go back to normal on its own.

Now, assuming your thoughts are like your breathing, which you could say they are, like the mind's breath in a sense, what happens to your thoughts in time – be they nervous ones, anxious ones, worried ones, excited ones? Exactly, you got it. After time, they move on to the next thought, and your feelings/experiences change, without actually doing anything at all.

Think about it, over the course of the day you experience a multitude of different thoughts, with resultant emotions and feelings. You are not, even if you suffer with your nerves, anxiety, depression or whatever, suffering all day with those emotions. Your emotions change naturally… with your thoughts. Like speedy breathing, where your breathing goes back to normal without doing anything, so do your thoughts and resultant emotions.

It gets better when you further explore this. Take the weather. I have lived in London, UK, all my life, where the weather seems to be more often than not gloomy and grey and we think that the blue sky is only there on the rare occasion. Well, that's wrong. The blue sky is always there, you just can't always see it.

Our default mode of being is actually like the blue sky. It's our thoughts that produce the grey clouds, but as our thoughts change regularly like our breathing, we can actually see the blue sky without doing anything as it's there all the time anyway.

Profound it seems I know, but it's true, and when you recognise it your thoughts will have a lesser power. In fact, when you recognise that thought is self-correcting like breathing you realise that it's not really your job to correct it.

I talked earlier about consciousness being one of the Three Principles. And once we 'get it' or have that insight or lightbulb moment about our thoughts, our level of consciousness is raised, and what seems right to us changes, so do our beliefs, our priorities and behaviour.

One last parallel way of looking at this, which was offered to me by Ian Watson, one of the leading Three Principles practitioners here in the UK:

Thought is like the background (what goes on behind the scenes) of a magic trick. It fools us, as we don't know how it (the effect – feelings/emotions) had been created. But once we know how the trick is created, the trick doesn't fool us in the same way, or shouldn't.

The difference is, thought can create that illusion in the form of magic, or indeed mayhem, in our own perception of reality! But **we** are the magician – the one creating the magic or mayhem, *and* we're the one experiencing it (which wouldn't happen if we were actual magicians as we'd know the trick and how it's done!). So now you know how your own illusory tricks are done, are you still going to be fooled?

What then does this mean in the context of Cojones?

Well, firstly, now that you know you are the architect of your own illusions and the negative outcomes you create with your thoughts, will you let them (the bad ones I mean) get in the way of you *doing* something to get a result you want? I would certainly expect not.

The point is, and what is different from the earlier chapter on TA, NLP and CBT, is that the reality is you don't actually have to change anything. In fact, this understanding means you can literally do anything you want to. You want to apply for a type of job, you want to ask that girl on a date, you want to set up that business, you want to tell your boss what you think of him, or whatever it is, you now know what role thought can play in limiting and stopping you.

And here's the thing, the more you *think* about the particular thought that's preventing you from taking whatever action you need or want to, the more energy you give to the thought, thus making it more powerful, and more likely debilitating. We've just seen that like speedy breathing, thought slows down to its natural pace without doing anything, so in reality, you don't need to analyse or judge the thought in any way. It's just a thought.

You're probably shouting at me now, saying, "But you said we could consciously do stuff to lessen the strength of our thoughts" by using the techniques of the previous chapter. Well, yes and no. What I am saying is that when you deeply understand the Three Principles you'll know that your thoughts and experiences will come and go. But, I say that if you're not ready for that insight into the Three Principles, and time is of the essence, you may need tools to push you to **do** whatever it is you want, without delay. Because yes, the debilitating and preventative thoughts will go, but I can't give you the timescale of when, and by then you may have missed the opportunity of whatever it is you want to do.

In the long term, by grasping this understanding you will likely need the interventions I gave you in the previous chapter less and less, but certainly in behaving according to the Cojones Code, taking on the Cojones mindset, the interventions of CBT, or the meta model of NLP, will hopefully, consciously get you from A to B, and importantly, without delay.

Of course, once your consciousness has been raised, when that lightbulb moment comes (when you aren't thinking or *trying* to have one) in 'getting' the Three Principles, you will need those interventions less and less, and be able to be more courageous, more bold and audacious, more naturally.

CHAPTER 7:

THE COJONES TEN COMMANDMENTS

OK, now we have all the more technical theory out of the way, it's time to really explore and take on board my own unique theories on growing a pair and living by the Cojones Code.

You see, I'm 47 years old at this point, and I have done many things that are the antithesis of Cojones, but I have also done many ballsy things, and through my own lightbulb moments, my own understanding of myself in how I have done stuff, as well as my study of others doing stuff too, along with psychological study of it all, I have realised there should be a few rules that act as a strong foundation to my theories of being bold, audacious and authentic.

Whether you are a religious person or not, I think it is fair to say that the original Ten Commandments supposedly given by the Almighty to Moses in biblical times offer a healthy guidebook for people to live by for there to be some sort of law and order in the human world.

I'm not going to get all religious or political on you, believe me – I could, but I won't, but personally I think that the world would be a terrible place if we didn't have the Ten Commandments as a guideline.

It's possible that without them the accepted moral code of what's considered right or wrong wouldn't be there for people to follow. Now I know that there's still murder, adultery, stealing etc etc in the world, but hey, the speed limit on the motorways here in the UK, as per the Highway Code, is 70mph. Yes, people go over 70mph, but people know they are breaking the law. What speed would people go if there were no guidelines/law? Certainly a lot more than 70mph, maybe 80mph, 90mph and who knows what upper limit, with possibly rather dangerous consequences.

By setting guidelines and rules, whilst the laws can and are broken, most people know they must adhere to them in some shape or form and normally do so. I know most people don't and will not adhere to my Cojones Ten Commandments, but once you see them and follow them, at least to some degree, you will become more authentic, more real, and more ballsy, which will help propel you towards whatever target you want for yourself.

Time to change your code for living then, and for the better!

Commandment 1: Say It As It Is

Do you go through life reluctant to express yourself and your feelings to others, be they work colleagues, family, friends and foes? Why?

What exactly are you afraid of? Making a fool of yourself, insulting someone, losing friends, rejection, love, popularity, loneliness? The reasons cover such vast ground that they are endless, but in any situation that relates to you, I'd like to ask you the question: "Why are you not saying it as it is?"

The truth is, if you follow this commandment, whether people like you for it or not, they will certainly learn to respect you for it.

It is well documented that keeping emotions inside and not diffusing them in some way is bad for your physical health, and stress on the body is the resultant factor. Why live that way?

There are literally millions of examples, but I'm going to take some classics that relate to Cojones in a few contexts.

In a relationship: This doesn't have to be an amorous relationship by the way, it can be any kind. But let's look at the romantic one.

Your boyfriend or girlfriend is taking you for granted, you start to feel used and not appreciated, and it's making you feel very unhappy. Actually, based on what we discussed in Chapter 5, no one can make you unhappy, it is your thinking behind it, but evidently the situation isn't working for you, so do you stay frustrated and upset? Many do, and live with these things as if they have to accept the status quo. But no, you don't.

This commandment doesn't demand you go and get into a confrontation or row, as there are linguistic and communication softeners that keep the mood and the interaction smooth.

So, it doesn't mean you go and say, "You bastard, you've been using me like a piece of old furniture, how dare you?" No, no, no, no, no.

But if you said something like, "I would be really grateful if we could have a chat, as there are a few things that are on my mind, and I think it would help our relationship if we could discuss them." A bit convoluted I know, but a softer approach. There's more than one way to 'skin a cat'. Sorry, animal lovers.

I'm not going to go into too much excess detail as to your whole chat, but if you get things off your chest, in the right way, it would likely ease some of that pain of holding on to it, and may give your relationship a welcome boost. Who knows, it might even be your lucky night tonight!

In the workplace: Your immediate superior is bossing you around, constantly giving you jobs to do that are outside your remit. You can't, and don't really want to, take on work that is meant for someone else, which means regularly staying late, for no more money. Yet you are afraid to rock the boat and create an atmosphere.

I hear this a lot. Or emotional bullying in another way, from colleagues who want to ensure they exert their superiority to make themselves feel important or whatever it may be. And you find it tends to be people who are good at their job (the one they should be doing) but are afraid to as this commandment says Say It As It Is.

I've heard all the excuses before as to why you can't open your mouth. But you are unhappy about the status quo, so to make it better you have to follow the commandment and grow a pair and speak up. Again, there are softeners to use to prevent a full-scale row, but I tell you what, if you are polite, firm and express yourself the right way, and show that you will not be a victim, you will likely feel a whole lot better, and work will be a better and happier place to go to in the morning. Unless you do night shifts!

I've taken a couple of classic contexts, and a couple of common scenarios, but whatever context or situation, to feel free, and true to yourself, you have to Say It As It Is. Remember those 'softeners' though.

Commandment 2: End Political Correctness - It's Simply Lying

Most people dislike or are at least critical of politicians. Why? Well, apart from never being happy regardless of any good that might have been done, we are, as human beings, much better at finding wrong than right, and the fact is that most people believe that politicians are liars. But I don't want to talk about the out and out lies they commit by promising to do one thing and then doing the other. I'm talking about their inability to be forthright in what they say in case they cause a modicum of offence. I'm aware that this is a strong parallel to the first commandment, but here's a couple of examples.

Tim Farron, when he was leader of the Liberal Democrats Party here in the UK, would not, despite continued questioning on the subject, admit that he was against gay marriage because of his strong religious beliefs. But why? Most people knew what his beliefs were, but he evaded the question, papered around it, and actually made us dislike him more.

What about more recently, when the Conservative politician and devout Christian Jacob Rees-Mogg was questioned on his belief that abortion was unacceptable after a woman had been raped? He simply constantly avoided the direct answer. They all do it, and we hate them for it.

But what about the opposite? What about politicians who do say what they really think?

There are a few of those, but how about the former leader of the United Kingdom Independence Party (UKIP) Nigel Farage? He, more often than not, said things according to his beliefs and built up an extraordinary following, so large that he was able to almost single-handedly bring about a referendum on Brexit – Britain's exit from membership of the European Union.

Again, I don't want to get political but much of his popularity was due to him **not** being politically correct. He said it how he saw it, rather than lying to himself and others. In fact, that is actually the core of this commandment. Why lie? I'm no saint and have done many stupid things in my life, but I would say lying has tended to not be one of them. Lying to me is not only cheating others, but cheating oneself, and I struggle with that I am proud to say.

There are of course many I know who say that they hate Farage for being so forthright, as he comes across abrasive in his views, but you can't have your cake and eat it. Of course, there are softeners one can use to enable the point to be put across with honesty and forthrightness in a better manner, but being politically correct, on the face of it, is simply lying, and why would anyone like to be lied to?

In my teens, when I asked a girl out and she said "Can we just be friends?" I hated that. We all know that they meant "You're aren't my type, love" – but friends? I had plenty of them, male peers of course, so why would I want any more? Did we ever stay friends? Of course not. Did they ever want to be friends'? Of course not. They were being politically correct. Lying basically.

So if you want to live authentically, then stop all this political correctness. Stop lying.

It actually seems the whole of political correctness has gripped society to such a degree that we can't make jokes, or even say the most natural and normal things without the PC (political correctness) brigade throwing their toys out of the pram.

Only the other week, I read that London Underground will not address people on the public address systems by a "Good morning ladies and gentlemen" as it would be offensive to transgender people, and is to be changed to "Good morning everyone." The world's gone mad. It's just laughable.

I would consider myself a sensitive bloke, to myself and others, but this fear of offending has been driven to ridiculous extremes that we have to walk on eggshells all the time now.

Well, *ladies and gentlemen,* not according to the Cojones Code. Start to be upfront, honest, and not only will people actually respect you for it, you will respect yourself for it. That doesn't mean being rude, as there are a number of ways to express oneself honestly, it just means be bloody honest, for heaven's sake.

Commandment 3: Like Nike, except 'FFS' Just Do It

I'm sure all of you know that the Nike slogan is 'Just Do It'.

I think it's brilliant. Very affirmative, and a call to action. Remember, at the start of the book I told you the one main thing I learned from my attending a personal development course is that 'the universe applauds action not thought'.

True true words, and Nike's world famous slogan underlines this.

Apologies if anyone, and particularly those at Nike, feels I am plagiarising a little, but the Cojones Code goes one step further. Yes, the third commandment is Like Nike, except 'FFS' Just Do It.

I am, as you know by now, less politically correct than Nike, so have gone in a little more bullish using FFS. I'm assuming you know what that means? If you are familiar with modern-day texting, or social media 'geek speak', then you'll know what it means. I'm not so keen to use outright expletives in this book, so here's my best offering of it: 'For Fxxk's Sake'. I presume no further explanation is necessary.

Anyway, it means take action, *Carpe Diem.*

The previous few chapters have gone into detail about how best to get yourself into the gear of 'doing', so I'll not harp on too much here, but this commandment is at the heartbeat of Cojones. In fact, this commandment is at the heartbeat of all the other commandments, because it can be said that without applying this one you'll have less chance of achieving the others – the first two above that you've just read, as well as subsequent ones. What this means is that anything you want to do, anything you want to say, anything you want to be, will start with this commandment.

Of course, as the UK's number one sports promoter, Barry Hearn, who we'll talk about more later, said to me in a *Cojones Icons* interview on Cojones TV (the Cojones YouTube channel), all the risks he takes are calculated ones. But you will know what it is you want to do in any context, so whilst this commandment can be a tad flippant, ultimately if you want to do anything you will have to take the plunge, so at that point I command you to 'FFS' Just Do It'.

There's a famous saying which is so right, and I wish I'd adhered to it 20 years ago: 'You will regret more what you don't do than what you did do.' Do you really want to live with that regret? I'm sure the answer is no, so the answer lies wholly with this commandment which is at the root of Cojones.

Commandment 4: No Moaning. No one Wants a Headache

Do you moan incessantly about the world not being good to you? Come on, be honest. Or do you have friends who constantly moan about their health, their job, their love life, and their life generally? I realise that much of the time spent with people is spent hearing their moans, and expressing one's own.

As you saw in the chapter on the Three Principles, our life is experienced from the inside out and **not,** as most people believe, from the outside in. That's right – from our own perceptions and attitudes. Your feelings and experiences are solely experienced via your thoughts, which means you are the captain of your own ship, and no outside weather can change your experience or course.

That being the case, and once you know that, you will be far less likely to blame anything exterior for what's going on in your life. Not only that, if you are like me and you get fed up with hearing people's moaning, then quit moaning yourself. I'm trying, and believe me, if I can so can you! And nowadays I realise I simply don't have time to waste listening to friends and family moan, complain and blame. It's time to take responsibility for your own life, and that also means not carrying everyone else's crap on your shoulders either.

Think about it like this. Taking action, being bold, audacious and authentic means taking life by the scruff of the neck. If you moan all the time, or surround yourself with people who moan, you are simply blocking the path to living. This commandment is there so that you pinch yourself next time you moan, and instead start bringing the Cojones Code into your life, based on the findings and advice of this book.

If you embrace the Cojones Code you won't moan, you'll notice more how much of your time has been spent on this futile waste of the most valuable resource we have access to: TIME. Remember, money comes and goes, but time only goes, so stop giving yourself and others, as well as letting others give you, a splitting headache by moaning.

Enough already!!

Commandment 5: Be You, Nobody Else Will

Part of living by the Cojones Code is being authentic.

We've discussed how being politically correct is lying and utterly inauthentic, and how 'saying it as it is' is part of the essence of living by the Cojones Code, so being yourself is of course the same, for heaven sake.

As humans, we tend to be brought up by our parents and guardians and conditioned by them to conform to societal and family norms. Now, some of these norms make sense for law and order purposes mostly, but what happened to individuality? It is variety that is the spice of life. If we all did exactly the same thing, had exactly the same interests, jobs, cuisine, life would be very, very boring indeed.

So why is society, as well as often those close to us, so intent on trying to minimise individuality?

I don't know about you, but I happen to like experiencing different things, going to different countries, seeing different cultures, trying different food etc, I presume you do too. That's respecting and celebrating others' way of life and collective individuality. So why not uphold your own individuality? We are all made of different shapes, skin colours, hairstyles and colours, height, weight, talents, thoughts and beliefs. Everyone should be proud of their own.

No one could play football like Diego Maradona, a man who is arguably the greatest ever, but as a 5'5" man, he was never going to win the Olympic high jump was he? But we could all appreciate the talent he had for football. His individual talent to play the world's most popular sport so amazingly.

So what I'm saying is whatever or however you are, be proud of that. If anyone has a problem with that – tough, it is solely their problem. If you're not doing them any harm, then hold your head up high for what you are. In a free society we don't have to dress like everyone else, behave like everyone else, look like everyone else, have the same ability as everyone else. We're all just flesh and bone, and if you can't be yourself, you can't be authentic, and ultimately be happy.

I saw an interview with Caitlyn Jenner, the woman who changed sex from being Bruce Jenner, the former Olympic Decathlon Gold Medallist. As a man, he didn't feel true to himself, he didn't feel authentic, so went against most of society's frowns and beliefs as to what is right and changed sex, so that he, or she as it is now, could be herself, and apparently is much happier for it. Well done to Caitlyn Jenner. I am not interested in her life, but I admire that quest to be oneself.

And being oneself often does take being bold and audacious, as we are often taught we have to consider others, and often before our own selves. Well, we don't actually. There is nothing more important than being true to yourself, as hard as that often is, but if you can make it a habit you will be happier, and things around you will be a lot better too.

Don't listen to most of the fake societal norms and memes, and adhere to this important Cojones Commandment.

Commandment 6: Throw the Dice and Play

This Cojones Commandment is very much about the 'doing'.

In Chapter 3 I related the story of how I met my future wife. I was on holiday in her country, Israel, and we stopped next to each other at traffic lights. I rolled down the window, asked her for directions and told her I was from England and needed to be shown around! I managed to get her telephone number and called her later. She wasn't interested at that time, but five months later, when I was back in the country, we met up and the rest is history. We have been married for ten years!

Now when I saw her, I wasn't thinking in the slightest she was my future wife, but I threw the dice and played. I seized the moment. I know, I know, you're probably saying to yourself 'I can't do those things'. Well you can, and you will, because if you don't, you're likely missing out.

All the Cojones Commandments are interlinked in some way, and again, if you use the interventions already highlighted in previous chapters, and in future ones, you'll be going some way to practising this type of action-orientated life for yourself.

So yes, here's another commandment to give you a rough guide to living.

Commandment 7: Don't Rip Up the Rule Book - Burn It Instead

Like I mentioned, these commandments have a number of crossovers, that much is obvious, but as I keep reiterating, if we were all the same, if there was no thinking differently from the rest, where would Mozart, Steve Jobs and the like be in the world?

If we didn't have people with Cojones, I can tell you the world wouldn't have evolved, developed and improved for the better. There would be no beautiful newly written music and even genres, no new technology, no new cures for disease, etc. Any revolution and evolution is derived from people thinking outside the box, being bold and having Cojones. In fact, I would go as far as to say Cojones is the foundation for the development of the world as we know it. All the people in history who have gone forward with their ideas or inventions or findings have shown and highlighted the Cojones Code to make themselves a success, and we've been lucky that they have.

Have you heard of the word gaudy? Well, it's derived from the work of the Catalan modernist Antoni Gaudi, best known for his architectural design of the church of Sagrada Familia in Barcelona. Today he is lauded, but while alive he was derided, with his work considered loud and not accepted (hence the word gaudy). But he stuck to his optimism and faith, largely in himself and his ideas, and this church particularly is one of the main tourist attractions in Barcelona and is revered. He's a classic example of someone who didn't just rip up the rule book. He literally burned it.

Many of Steve Jobs' ideas failed or were derided, but now Apple, at the time of writing, is the most valuable company in the world, with the famous original iPhone literally single-handedly changing everyone's lives.

Have you had ideas that you were sure were the makings of something, but because it didn't conform to so-called normality, you didn't move forward with them? I bet. Remember any great idea that isn't acted upon to fruition is nothing more than a dream, and it doesn't matter if you fail, as the only failure in life is the failure to try.

I've posed the question, where would the world be without some of the above people and more, who have shown balls and Cojones?

But, here's another question, can you imagine where the world could be if even more people had the Cojones to bring their ideas to fruition? Possibly light years ahead of where we are in every sense.

I therefore encourage you (within the legal limits of course) to think outside the box. If you want to be the same as everyone you will still be valuable as a human being, but if you think differently from others that makes you potentially invaluable. To do that entails going against the grain, and adhering to this commandment.

Commandment 8: Don't Ask - Don't Get. So Ask and You May

Do you expect everything to just fall into your lap? Well, I've got some sobering news for you if you do: it simply won't. If you want something in this world, apart from going out and getting it (following the Cojones Code), you may need to ask for a number of things.

- If you want the sale? You've got to ask for it.

- If you want a pay rise? You've got to ask for it.

- If you want the date? You've got to ask for it.

Whatever it may be. Even if you want your food hotter in a restaurant, you've got to ask for it.

Many people, particularly people here in England, haven't got the balls, the Cojones to ask for what they want. Why?

Cojones includes a number of things as you've witnessed already, but having the guts, the confidence, the boldness, and sometimes the outright audacity to ask for what you want, even if you think you've got little chance of getting it, will certainly and massively increase your chances. In most cases, the worst anyone can answer you with is a simple No.

The greatest failure in life is indeed the failure to try, and that includes asking for what you want. I mean, what is it you are actually afraid of? The answer should be nothing, but whatever it is, much of what we discussed in Chapters 4 and 5 will help you negate those blockages.

I was given some limiting beliefs growing up, or I should say, I took on those limiting beliefs, about what's possible and what's impossible, and most of it was a load of garbage. My dear mother was very superstitious often telling me, "Don't put your keys on the table", "Don't spill salt without chucking some over your left shoulder." It's utter nonsense, but we humans seem to adhere to this kind of stuff, and in the same way we follow society's propriety and conditioned limitations to the point of superstition.

To hell with that. You want to live life to the full, you want to get somewhere, you have to do what it takes, and that includes asking when you need to.

One of my interviewees in my *Cojones Icons* series on Cojones TV was the well-known British showbiz agent Jonathan Shalit. When he was young he identified the job he wanted, and found out from outside the office building of that company which one was the firm's boss's office, and which window!

He ended up giving his CV to the window cleaner, with a letter **asking** for a job. He got the job.

He thought outside the box, and **asked.** He didn't fear a no answer, and was happily surprised when he got a yes. I suppose it's no wonder he's successful in what he does, as he follows the Cojones Code, and yes, he knows that if you don't ask, you don't get. In his example, he asked, and he did get.

Commandment 9: Fear No One, Approach Anyone

We are all human beings. Well, if you are reading this I presume you are. All of us, like anyone, bleed if we are cut. That's right, we are made of the same flesh and blood. No one is better or worse than you or me. It is only our perception of their power, status, wealth etc that makes us fearful of them. I can tell you, I don't care if someone is the president of the United States, the owner of

Microsoft, or even the eventual publisher of this book. I don't fear any of them. And why should I?

We can respect people for their achievements, but fear them? Absolutely no way. Fear is only something dreamt up in your own mind. If your perception was different you wouldn't fear them, and would have no problem approaching them. OK, I may not approach some crazed gunman, or a mugger with a knife, but I'm not talking about that.

In this world we are again taught to see people in different hierarchal ways, much of that is the fault of the media, who often put Neanderthal so-called reality TV stars up on a pedestal, or film stars because they acted well in a film. Big bloody deal. I couldn't care less. What's important is to not be afraid of anyone if you need to approach them for whatever reason.

One of the things this book teaches is the notion of the Yiddish word chutzpah, meaning outrageous audacity, and like the story earlier about Jonathan Shalit, he didn't fear that company boss when adopting a unique and bold way to approaching him, and ultimately got the job. He simply wanted something and he went for it.

Part of having chutzpah, which is a big component of the Cojones Code, is ultimately knocking on the doors you need to in order to get them opened. No one is going to do that for you, and you may have to knock hard to be heard, but if you have fear of anyone you'll be unlikely to do it.

When I began my *Cojones Icons* series on the Cojones TV YouTube channel, which was actually meant as a research tool for my theories, I had no backing from a major broadcasting corporation like the BBC or Sky. I used some of what I would call social engineering to get the direct phone numbers of my target interviewees, and phoned them direct to convince them to be interviewed by me.

By the way, using Cojones for sales is vital, as a major rule is always 'wherever possible go direct to the decision maker' which is what I did. I went direct to some of the Cojones Icons, like Nigel Farage, Alastair Campbell, Judge Rinder (big British names) and pitched them direct. I showed no fear, as I don't fear them. Yes, they had something I wanted from them, their stories about their successful mindsets, but fearful I was not.

Whether you are applying for a job, want that bank loan, want that girl, or boy, fear needs to be banished – immediately.

I repeat, no one regardless of their so-called social status, wealth, fame is better or worse than us. If you have any thoughts that they are, get rid of them now (some of the techniques in earlier chapters will help, as will those in later ones).

If you are going to live, to act, to behave and go for it, living by the Cojones Code, then I command you to Fear No One, and if you need to Approach Anyone.

Commandment 10: Be a Shepherd not a Sheep

Talk about leaving the best until last. OK, maybe not the best, but certainly the most important. Because it is this commandment that underpins Cojones. It certainly underpins success to a huge degree.

No one has ever achieved great things by being the same as everyone else. They have done so by being different and embracing that, such as:

- Top revolutionary businessmen like Steve Jobs

- Top politicians like Margaret Thatcher, Tony Blair, or even Nigel Farage

- Top guitarists like Eric Clapton, Slash or Angus Young

- Top inventors like Alexander Graham Bell or Sir James Dyson

The list goes on and on, but none of these people would have got to where they are or were without having the boldness to be different, to try different things, and feel brave enough to stand out from the rest. The world evolves by having people such as those mentioned, as they are willing to step out of their and society's comfort zone and make it bigger, therefore making things better for the rest of us.

How do you want to be?

By the way, I do not have a problem if you want to be like the rest. Many people do, and simply want the easiest life possible. That's fine. But if you're reading this book, then presumably you have an interest at the very least with what separates the few from the rest, and it is this one final commandment.

And I'm not saying be different for the sake of it. That's not it. It's about if you have ideas, have aims, dreams, actions you'd like to take, then you will do so by daring to be different. By choosing your own path and not being a sheep by following the same path trodden by every Tom, Dick and Harry.

There will be friends and family who will 'pooh-pooh' your thoughts, ideas and dreams, but remember well what Albert Einstein said: "Great spirits have often encountered violent opposition from mediocre minds."

There's another wonderful quote, and actually there are many that uphold this commandment, but how about this one from Robert H Schuller: "I would rather attempt something great and fail than attempt nothing at all and succeed."

I know which I would prefer.

I've done a number of things related to my Cojones motivational entertainment brand, and many have said, "You can't do that" or almost laughed at my theories and ideas. In fact, I try these days to distance myself from people whom I know largely through their own addiction to the ordinary or frustration at it and who want to see others remain in a similar mould. Either stay away from those people completely, or don't share your ideas, dreams or actions with them, just have enough conviction to keep going.

One last great quote regarding this: "I think the reward for conformity is that everyone likes you, except yourself." Rita Mae Brown

So, if you really aim to live in a special way and do something extraordinary then this commandment **must** be adhered to. You will have to be a shepherd not a sheep, and I command you, or less dictatorially advise you, to stick to it if you really want whatever it is you are after.

Conclusion to the Cojones Ten Commandments

The word commandment is made slightly tongue in cheek, as of course I am not the Almighty, and only a product of the Almighty like you.

But having observed and devised my theories on the Cojones way of life, living by the Cojones Code, which is to Grow a Pair for Success and authenticity, then if you adhere to these commandments, and I mean live by them, you are bound to live a fuller life.

CHAPTER 8:

SELF-ESTEEM AND THE NECESSITY FOR COJONES

I have heard it said by a famous expert on this subject that self-esteem is the reputation we gain within ourselves.

As we have touched upon in this book already, much of what we do, or actually what we don't do, is down to the beliefs we have about ourselves. When we are children we learn pretty much everything from our parents, closest peers and teachers, and the messages we receive from them literally instil into us what we feel we are capable of.

Actually, my theory is that without the most basic self-esteem and confidence, we wouldn't even be able to do the most basic of things, like cross the road or leave our house in the morning. Of course, this isn't a book about basic self-esteem, because if it were it would be a book more about psychology, which it isn't, and in any case, this book assumes you are able to do the most basic activities involving some degree of self-esteem and confidence. At the same time, let me give you a little anecdote about how self-esteem can be harmed.

Mike was a talented tennis player, and at the age of 12 played in a club tournament. His dad came to watch his match at which he was really excited. He won the match but lost a second set tie-break when he had opportunities to win. An excited winner was Mike, who after the match went straight to his dad for approval and recognition for his win and efforts. Mike's dad said, "But how did you lose that second set?" Mike's heart sank.

All his good work was shattered by the shroud of negativity for losing that second set. That kind of negativity was continuous and, needless to say, Mike was subsequently so scared of anything less than perfection that he found it harder to win in the future, and eventually gave up the game that he had a talent for.

So most of us, through all sorts of experiences in some way similar to these, can have our self-esteem and confidence knocked, thus preventing us from doing all sorts of things in our life despite our talents. What a shame.

Now of course we can blame Mike's dad for destroying his tennis career, and yes, when we are young we are particularly affected by the responses (in TA terms, the negative strokes) of our parents and peers. But there does come a time when we're older, once we have the realisation that we don't have to be the victim of others' limiting messages, as to whether we are going to be or do something or nothing *because of*, and alternatively can have the new mindset of doing something *in spite of*.

What I want you to do is the latter. The time has come to do, be or say something *in spite of*. And when I say in spite of, I mean in spite of any restrictive limiting messages you received. Remember, most of the messages received are from your parents, family and peers and these are most likely to be the ones they themselves received from their parents' own history of negativity, and knowing that alone can give you the catalyst you need to act *in spite of.*

That's a vital message from me to you in adopting Cojones in your life, by opposing your own default behaviours and actions. Start immediately by saying you will live your life the way you want to, to do what you want to, to be what you want to *in spite of* your history and messages.

I know it sounds a lot easier than I'm making it out to be, but most changes in behaviour start with a decision. Your own decision to do what is necessary. So make the decision **now** to live *in spite of* and not *because of.*

And let's not forget, it's so much easier to live, do and be *because of*, as it's swimming with the current, but let me tell you, if you **decide** you will live, be and do *in spite of* you will be swimming with the current, as you have the power to change the direction of the stream.

Now, if you remember the chapter on the Three Principles, you will know that some people with the same upbringing will live *because of* and some *in spite of*, it effectively proving that it is all based on how any individual *thinks* about the messages received.

In fact, whether you live, be or do according to one of these two directions is based solely on your thoughts around these messages. Knowing that alone will enable you to realise it is down to you which of the *in spite of* or *because of* positions you decide to take. It's actually very simple when you *think* about it.

Taking it further still, you've now realised you are the architect of your own experiences via your thoughts, so you can choose which self-esteem direction to go in – *because of* or *in spite of.* Now, you can in relation to your self-esteem, follow the Cojones Ten Commandments, as follows:

Commandment 1 - Say It As It Is

My parents often said to me that "Children should be seen and not heard." What utter nonsense, and what better way to stifle the free child (part of the Child ego state in TA) and stop them expressing themselves.

But once you have had the realisations like the above, and decide to take the more effective route, you will now be more equipped to obey this commandment. Your self-esteem will improve, as you will now stop hiding and expressing your true beliefs and feelings.

Commandment 2 - End Political Correctness - It's Simply Lying

This one only has relevance in the self-esteem context insofar as if you didn't care about being judged or what others thought, which has much to do with self-esteem, you wouldn't need to be so politically correct. Bottom line as in Commandment 1 – by following the *in spite of* direction you will be much more your own man (or woman), a good sign of healthy self-esteem.

Commandment 3 - Like Nike, except 'FFS' Just Do It

Obey this commandment, and the more you have a go, the more your self-esteem will improve. Remember the universe applauds action and **choosing** the *in spite of* self-esteem route means you will 'Just Do It'.

Commandment 4 - No Moaning. No one Wants a Headache

Moaning is remaining in the *because of* camp, and is a symptom of it. Once you decide to be in the *in spite of* camp, you will not allow yourself to moan. Actually you just won't moan, period! Effectively you will have gone the other way, so you will moan a lot less, if at all. Thank goodness for that eh?!

Commandment 5 - Be You, Nobody Else Will

By doing the above, you will be more inclined to be **you.** You'd have lost a lot of your inhibitions and limiting thoughts and resultant behaviours. And now you know for sure, there's no reason you shouldn't be you.

So, nice to meet you. The real **you** that is.

Commandment 6 - Throw the Dice and Play

By taking the *in spite of* route, you will naturally decide to throw the dice more. Your self-esteem will again go up a notch as a result of doing so, so it's a double whammy. Remember you've decided to take a new path to healthier self-esteem. So, following this commandment will empower you. But make sure it is calculated. As I don't mean gamble, willy nilly.

Commandment 7 - Don't Rip Up the Rule Book - Burn It Instead

If you've lived the *because of* self-esteem route, then your rule book is based on, if not wholly copied from, others' negative messages. With the new way, you are sticking two fingers up at that, and with all the above you will be more likely to follow this commandment. But, like the rest of the commandments, obey them and your self-esteem will improve, and your life will become empowered as you suddenly make many of your own rules.

Commandment 8 - Don't Ask - Don't Get. So Ask and You May

Because of people are afraid to ask for the things they want, as they are afraid of rejection, or a no answer. If you have **decided** to live, be or do the route of *in spite of,* your self-esteem would be healthier, and you'll be far more likely to go for it, and open your mouth, meaning asking for what you want. And doing it more often means your self-esteem will be improving at the same time. Another double whammy!!

Commandment 9 - Fear No One, Approach Anyone

Similar to number 8. Because you will be more empowered after **deciding** you will live, be and do in the self-esteem direction of *in spite of,* you will fear a lot less. You will have less tendency to reach for the excuse book, meaning you will do what it takes to get the results you want.

Commandment 10 - Be a Shepherd not a Sheep

As you have likely noticed, pretty much all of the commandments are intertwined to some degree, and with improved self-esteem you will be more capable of obeying the commandments. In the same way, if you literally obeyed the commandments your self-esteem would go up a notch.

Most people with low self-esteem are incapable of being someone who leads the way, but when you **decide** to be *in spite of* in the self-esteem stakes, and set your own agenda, you will not need to follow others all the time, you will be far more inclined to lead the way yourself.

I Repeat – Double Whammy

You can see now that with greater self-esteem and **deciding** to be in the *in spite of* camp, and taking that stance, your self-esteem will rise naturally. In the same way, if you 'obey' the Ten Commandments verbatim, then your self-esteem and confidence will again rise up a notch or two... or three.

They are all double whammies, and further underlines how relevant this whole subject is to performance, results and living authentically and more happily. Therefore, if you really want to live the Cojones way by following the Cojones Code, and do things in your life that most others daren't, what you need is effectively 'supercharged' self-esteem.

Decide now to live, do and be *in spite of* your past experiences, and your self-esteem will immediately improve.

By also realising that only your thoughts create your experience, and actually nothing external, and then obeying the commandments, your self-esteem will improve massively. But the good part is that by doing all this the habit of doing, being and living your way will improve your lot.

And yes, the circle of empowerment will continue to gain pace, as this habit of taking the above action will become natural and default.

I don't think you can lose.

CHAPTER 9:

COJONES ICONS

We've already touched upon how from our earliest years as infants we learn from and copy others including all the positive and negative stuff. From the cradle onwards, we literally learn through copying, imitating and modelling our nearest influencers, parents, teachers and peers.

In fact, not just when we are infants and youngsters do we learn and pick up things from others, but as adults too we continue to learn, form opinions and beliefs all the time from our peers, studies, and of course the media.

For those who want to know more about the footprint our environment and messages have on us, I recommend the book

The Virus of The Mind by Richard Brodie, which actually demonstrates 'mind viruses' as a science, called Memetics.

For the moment though, let's keep it a little more basic to say that 'the apple doesn't fall far from the tree', and that our learned behaviours and actions are adopted through copying others. So why not, if you want to adopt the Cojones Code into your life, consciously look for others to learn from.

That's right, others who have used their own Cojones to be successful in whatever it is they have been successful in. Or even others who have Cojones-type qualities or behaviours that you would benefit from having, even if you don't like or don't necessarily respect that person, and you will see what I mean further on. Just warning you!

You see, as my mother always said, everyone has some good qualities, and in that way there are people I literally deplore, yet admire some of their capabilities or qualities, and want a bit of what they've got for myself. To that end, below I have given you a few Cojones Icons you and I may not necessarily like, but with an open mind can learn from in some shape or form.

In fact, using this open-minded approach is exactly how I have deepened my own theories of results, success and authenticity (yes, Cojones) by learning from and modelling some of my own Cojones Icons.

There are of course numerous people that spring to mind who in some shape or form have demonstrated Cojones to some degree, which I'd like to learn and adopt for my own life. What about you? It could be a friend, a colleague, a politician, a sportsman or sportswoman, entrepreneur, actor, or whoever. If they have qualities that you can learn from to make you more bold and audacious, it would benefit you to do so.

I must repeat that you don't have to like the person. You can even hate them. But if they have something you would like a bit of, then there's nothing wrong in trying to model that something.

For now, I'm going to come up with a few of my own, who subsequent to me admiring *some* of their qualities to some degree and in *some* shape or form, I have interviewed for my Cojones TV YouTube channel, enabling me to peer into their mindset and yes, learn from them. Before I do so though, I would like to point out that different people have used their Cojones in different ways, and in my findings, as well as my interview series, I have chosen subjects who have used theirs for some of the following:

- Entrepreneurship

- Being audacious

- Speaking out

- Political campaigning against the odds

- Sporting achievement

- Being different and/or being oneself

- Thinking outside of the box – creativity

- Brushing off criticism and tenacity

- Integrity

The above are just a few, as the list is far more exhaustive.

Can you think of any others?

Arsène Wenger - Cojones for Implementing Change

You will have read the story early in this book about how I finally got to interview Arsène Wenger, and for those who are slow readers and not from the UK, this is the man who spent 22 years as the manager/coach of Arsenal Football Club, and is renowned for changing the face of the game of football (soccer) in this country. A man who changed the training methods of players, coaches, the diets, the way the game is played with a fluid attacking style, and someone who is truly revered the world over.

The last few years of his reign as manager of the club were a little strained, as many thought he had gone stale somewhat, but nevertheless he still stuck to his steadfast principles. The irony is that when he arrived in England, the typical British media labelled him 'Arsène Who?' as no one had heard of him. Even his new football rivals tried to humiliate him on his arrival, questioning his credibility. That soon changed, as his methods extended the careers of the players in their 30s, and almost instantly created a team of champions, whilst playing an eye-catching and exciting brand of football.

Many people hate football, and I apologise for that, as there's another football 'icon' later in this chapter that I refer to, but it's irrelevant whether you love the game or hate it as it's about modelling the traits and qualities of a man who had the Cojones to completely change decades-old methods, doing it his way, according to his vision, with enormous success.

When I interviewed him he came across as a man who is utterly self-assured, despite admitting self-doubt at times, yet he was adamant that he was successful because firstly he had a key idea of what he wanted to do, as well as having the capacity to formulate it properly and make it understandable, whilst getting people (in his case his players) to own his ideas too.

As he put it to me, a mixture of the intellectual and practical. This is, in a way, a blueprint for business as well. We need to have our own key idea of what we want to do and then formulate it, and make it understandable and practicable. What came across when I interviewed him was that he was able to naturally do both, have an intellectual as well as a practical approach – a way to implement.

How can we learn from this? If we have our own strong idea or ideas of doing something, then moving it to fruition means us being able to formulate it, make it understandable and implementable.

This is what I call practical Cojones. Wenger was obviously utterly focused, but I believe he was able to ignore the noise and the doubters because he had conviction in his ideas, and knew exactly how to implement them. The combination of the two enabled him to go forward and create a winning formula for himself and his team, becoming a legend in the process and globally revered in the world of football.

He is nicknamed 'The Professor', and whilst this man has incredible intellect, I feel it is also for his ability to put a working formula into his work that has also given him that label/nickname.

If you have a practical working formula, then you will be far more able to implement your ideas into fruition. That working formula, if properly considered and practically thought out, will in itself give you the impetus, and enable you to develop the Cojones to go forward in whatever it is you seek to achieve.

David Walsh - Cojones to Speak Out

Now whilst David isn't a name everyone knows, he is the chief sports writer of the well-regarded British newspaper *The Sunday Times*, and you will most likely know him for his famous pursuit of cycling drugs cheat Lance Armstrong.

Lance Armstrong became infamous for fighting back to recovery from life-threatening cancer to win the Tour de France, the world's most gruelling cycle race, not just once but seven times in a row. A man who was lauded as a hero wherever he went because of his heroic story, going from being at death's door to the main man on the Tour de France, the world's toughest sports competition. Then raising hundreds of millions of dollars for his Livestrong cancer charity, mixing with royalty, having film star girlfriends, etc etc.

But all along, David Walsh, a highly respected journalist, knew Armstrong was cheating and using performance-enhancing drugs to win. Armstrong always denied it of course, continuing to live the lie as a national (actually an international) hero, when all along it was just one massive sham.

David Walsh is a man whose integrity and professionalism never let up, as he knew all along that Armstrong was pulling the wool over the world's eyes, and David, in the name of honesty and integrity as a human being, as well as for his love of sport, was determined to expose this grandest of hoaxes. Thirteen years of pursuit was what it took Walsh to eventually be revered for his work as a legendary journalist after exposing arguably the biggest sporting controversy and story in the history of world sport. Throughout all those years, David was unafraid to let everyone know the truth. **To speak out and say it as it was.**

During those 13 years, Armstrong was untouchable. There were people who knew the truth, but David was one of the only people at the time to dare say it, despite the fact the cycling world and fellow journalists were against him. There were as well the people who had invested time and money in Lance Armstrong and his cycling team, and all who were taken in by the Armstrong story of hope who didn't want it shattered to pieces, regardless of whether he was cheating or not.

David told me a story of when he was in a queue at an airport. A few people in front of him stood a man wearing a Livestrong band around his wrist. David subsequently made his way over to the man and told him straight, "That bracelet represents Lance Armstrong – he's a fraud, and you shouldn't be supporting him." The guy looked at him as if were an alien.

David confirmed that people wanted it to be true so closed out the logic!

So big was the story, a Hollywood movie was made called *The Program*, based on Walsh's book *My Pursuit of Lance Armstrong*, with Walsh himself being played by the actor Chris O'Dowd.

Yet this was a story that Walsh had to endure, including being abandoned by his own professional peers who chose to be yes men, instead of pursuing the truth, being criticised in a despicable way by Armstrong himself, and David's employers being sued for several hundred thousand pounds, with his own reputation being questioned. However, he never wavered from the facts that he obtained, from the belief that he was right and most of the rest of the world were wrong, and saw it through to its rightful conclusion – Armstrong being stripped of his seven Tour De France titles, and Walsh achieving justice for the truth, his honesty and integrity.

I have such respect for the man himself and the Cojones he demonstrated in the name of integrity and speaking out. Living by the Cojones Code is about being honest and true to yourself, and he did exactly that.

When I began my own *Cojones Icons* series on my Cojones TV YouTube channel, he was one of the first people I wanted to interview, and when I talk to audiences about modelling Cojones Icons in some way, he is one of the first people I refer to.

So what did I learn from him? What qualities did he show to see his pursuit of Lance Armstrong through to its rightful conclusion?

Well firstly, I can quote David in the interview I did with him. He said that it wasn't gut instinct but gut conviction that he had, and he had the energy to carry it forward. He said he had no negative self-talk either, which is extremely helpful in going towards a mightily difficult goal. Due to his unquestionable conviction, evidence surfaced that strengthened it.

David was even verbally warned/threatened by one of Lance Armstrong's teammates, but he wasn't intimidated because he's not someone who thinks anything bad will happen to him – his words to me. He actually thinks the reverse. And most importantly, I will quote David verbatim now in what most struck me, and what I feel compelled me to model in him:

"If you think something isn't right, you have a duty to say something isn't right. Don't go with the flow. If you do that, even if you feel uncomfortable, people will notice. Good people, and support you."

Now of course, David's last statement referred partially to journalism, his vocation, but for sure it refers to life in general. So what qualities do you think David showed in the story? I'd say some of the following:

- Confidence to say it as it is or as he saw it
  (a Cojones Commandment)

- Tenacity

- Duty

- Integrity

- Self-belief

- Responsibility

- His positivity in the future

- Humility

I actually believe the last one helped him enormously. David, in my few dealings with him and the interview, is very humble, and I think it is that which has enabled him to go forward towards his goal of exposing the truth. Had David's ego been supersized and, indeed, his main driving force, he'd have done what he did for the wrong reasons, possibly not have received the support and help from others he talked about over his 13-year pursuit of Armstrong, and therefore may not have been so successful. I believe that humility gave him the conviction he talked to me about.

Some of David's qualities of course will be explored further later on, as we unravel the qualities of Cojones Icons that we would be well served to learn and to model, but I finish on David Walsh in what his message to myself and others is: "Stay true to your gut. Your belief."

Nigel Farage - Cojones for a Vision

If you're British, you will have had to be in hibernation for the last ten years to not know who this guy is.

He's not everyone's cup of tea being a politician, but he is arguably one of the most influential political figures in this country since Margaret Thatcher. I know there are others, and I don't want to get into a political debate with you, but you can't deny this man's impact on the UK, whether you think it has been for better or for worse. What I want to focus on is how he had the Cojones to do what he did, and what qualities he has and had in order to achieve it.

Firstly of course, just in case you have been in hibernation, I'm going to briefly remind you who this man is.

About 20 years ago, a new political party was born largely to oppose Britain's membership to the European Union. Farage was there from the start, becoming leader in 2006 for four years and then again in 2010 for another six years.

Arguably this man lifted this party and its cause by the scruff of the neck, leading them to become the biggest party in the European parliament. Perhaps most importantly, at least to them, it aimed to ensure the British government under David Cameron's Conservative party called a referendum on Britain's membership of the European Union.

Farage, so many claim, is responsible not only for the granting of the referendum but being one of the foremost campaigners for the UK voting for exit, otherwise colloquially called Brexit. An amazing achievement for a man leading a party effectively from nothing, to making a huge impact on the UK, whilst being in a political system (First Past the Post) that makes it much harder for minority parties to succeed. UKIP did, and largely because of Farage. And yes, Farage's extraordinary Cojones.

In my interview with Nigel for Cojones TV, here are some of things he revealed to me about his own Cojones.

He told me that his absolute belief on the issue of Brexit and the fact that he didn't see anyone else with the 'balls' to do it drove him forward.

I did ask him that whilst he seemed like a hugely confident man whether he ever had any self-doubt, to which he admitted humbly that he often asked himself 'am I up to it?' and that down moments arose when the adrenaline was not there. It goes to show you that when you look at people, however tough they seem, there's always that humbling fact that they also experience some doubts. We really are all human.

I was also very interested to know how he rode some of the most overwhelming criticism and accusations – and his answer? "You just have to brush yourself off and keep going – a thick skin is something you develop as you go along." And what was most poignant was that he admitted that if you want the big dream, as so many do, and he's met many of those who are ballsy and gutsy, but don't have the following quality to go with it – *patience*. His advice was very clear: "If you're gonna pursue a big dream, you need to be ballsy and strong *but* you won't do it overnight."

The above insight into the mind of a true Cojones Icon, whether you love him or loathe him, is without a doubt priceless advice for your own pursuit of a Cojones mindset.

Alastair Campbell - Cojones for Outside the Box Thinking and Openness

Another British Cojones Icon. And like Nigel Farage, for different reasons, not everyone's cup of tea.

Actually, he's pretty well known in foreign circles in the political world, as he was Tony Blair's spokesman, and Downing Street's press secretary during the Labour Party's greatest and most successful time in government. In fact, he is noted as being largely responsible for devising the strategy that saw Labour elected to power under their modern guise 'New Labour', as well as being re-elected two more consecutive times. Unheard of before in his party. He though was one of the main catalysts.

He is also a very successful journalist, broadcaster and author. A man whose CV is lit up with extraordinary successes, whilst at the same time suffering from depression and being a recovering alcoholic, making his success even more remarkable and, of course, admirable.

Again, you may not agree with his politics, but who cares. If we can learn from the side of his mindset that has led him to success, then indeed we should. Even if he is a mad Burnley Football Club fan. I know, that is very weird! Sorry, Burnley fans.

But seriously, here was a man with the Cojones to change the Labour Party's historical constitution, going against long-heralded Labour traditions, and was a major part in the branding of Labour to 'New Labour', allowing them to be enormously electable and successful. At the same time Alastair was battling his own demons, whilst being brave enough to be open about them at a time when being open about being an alcoholic and a sufferer of depression was considered taboo, and judged very negatively.

So here we have a man who has the Cojones to be utterly driven by his convictions, to be different in his approach (as he was with Labour), whilst being courageous enough to be open about his flaws. Let's be honest, we all have flaws, but Alastair Campbell did much to break the taboo of openly having the flaws he has, contributing to the greater acceptance in our society of these issues.

Yes, this is definitely someone who I consider to be a Cojones Icon, and someone we can learn from and model. I had the luck of interviewing Alastair for the *Cojones Icons* series on my YouTube channel, and here are some of the messages I, and hopefully others, were able to take from him in learning to adopt the Cojones Code. In fact, there are two main points that I took from Alastair which are so pertinent to the Cojones theory and way of life.

Here is a man who openly suffers from depression, yet managed to carry enormous pressure in terms of the positions he held, and I was curious as to how he managed to carry on and shoulder such responsibility particularly when times were tough mentally. It would seem, from his answer, that when he was at his lowest point ever, when he had his breakdown, that he realised a kind of self-generated mantra, so he could cope in the future. That was: "In tough times, I always compared it to my lowest point and said to myself it's not as bad as that."

Another, and perhaps most relevant, point is related to his record of being successful at pretty much anything he has done, be that politics, journalism, writing etc, and that when he has seen something that has tickled his fancy to do, and to try. He has done exactly that, and in his own words he told me the advice he'd give to anyone: "Don't let your default position be no, I can't do that. I said to myself I could have a go at that, so I say most people have got it within them to do something a bit special, so have a go and see how far you can get."

Great advice Alastair, thanks.

And that is why having Cojones Icons is so important, because not only can we try and model them, we can carry their messages around with us in the form of a parrot on our shoulder, by having their valid, tried and tested messages and formulas in our ear for when we need them for motivation. Useful, don't you think?

Barry Hearn - Cojones for Entrepreneurship

Depending on where in the world you live, you may or may not have heard of some or all of these names. But actually it doesn't really matter, because all of them stand for something that would be relevant in life, and to be learned from.

Barry is a working class bloke who made good and became the biggest sports promoter in the UK. His mother, a cleaner, embedded into him at a young age his amazing work ethic and encouraged him to train as an accountant. When he asked his mother why he should do that, her response was simply, "Because you never see a poor one." I'm not sure that's accurate, but it's advice he took and worked hard to become qualified.

Following on from that, a chance meeting with a prodigious talent in the game of snooker saw him make his foray into the sporting business world, and become a significant driving force behind snooker being the most watched sport in the UK in the 1980s.

Following on from that, he became a hugely successful boxing promoter, brought the pub game of darts to enormous popularity, as well as other sporting endeavours.

I wanted to interview him because of his Midas touch in whatever he seemed to turn his hand to. Also, having heard him speak before, I realised his mindset was totally 'yes can do' in true Cojones style.

So what's his secret? What came across was: 1) His belief in a hard-work ethic. 2) Despite the perception that he takes risks, and he does, they are calculated risks. 3) He hasn't got time to have a negative thought.

The first one is self-explanatory, and takes zero talent. He's saying that his attitude, rather than aptitude, is key, and that whatever he does he works damned hard at it.

The second one is also interesting, as he is perceived as someone who takes frivolous risks, yet, as he said, what people don't see is the research and work he puts in beforehand and behind the scenes to see whether his ideas are indeed viable. As he says, "If you do your homework, you'll pass the exam."

One thing's for sure in his reasoning behind his success. By doing all the background work, his project will have far less chance of failing.

The third one is slightly idealistic, as we all have negative thoughts, but what I got from him was that he knows that it is pointless to spend any time deliberating on them.

As one of my Cojones Icons, he has a great attitude, and one in which his qualities make for essential modelling.

Sarah Willingham - Cojones for Female Entrepreneurship

Whilst we live in a world of far greater equality amongst race, religion, sexuality and gender, certainly in the West inequality still exists, be that in pay, respect and standing for women in the world of commerce. Misogyny is still rife, and for sure, women in the world of employment, and even more so business and entrepreneurship, require guts, confidence, strength, and yes, the Cojones mindset.

There are of course many successful businesswomen, and in my desire to understand a little bit more about the inner psyche of one, I managed to secure an interview with Sarah Willingham.

If you live in the UK you may know her as one of the 'dragons' in the hit BBC television show *Dragons' Den*, where aspiring entrepreneurs with a grand business idea pitch it to a 'dragon' (a successful businessperson) to secure their financial investment as well as experienced input.

Sarah was one of the dragons for two years, and whilst coming across as naturally astute, always had a nice way about her, which I found when I was lucky enough to meet and chat to her. What was interesting about Sarah was how her curiosity from a young age about corporate brands found its way into business based on her passion for food, from running well-known restaurant chains to starting her own.

So, as a woman, no doubt she needed to have the guts and gusto to make it in the entrepreneurial world, to which she admitted. She was very forthright in how she turned that perceived restriction of her chances to make it on its head with the following mindset and snippets of wisdom:

"As a minority, you're fighting more because you're not part of the masses, but what I've always said to women is, in a room full of grey suits who are they going to remember? Be the person that stands out.

"Allow yourself to be the person that's different. I was good at my job, but who are they going to remember – someone who is good at their job, or someone who's a bit different who's good at their job?"

The interesting thing about Sarah is how honest she was about her own self-doubt that we all have. She admitted, "I have suffered from imposter syndrome my whole life – like when I was in the dragon's chair. It's very normal to have the negative self-talk, but anything I have done in my life, I ask what is my ultimate downside? If I felt I could handle that, I've gone ahead and done it."

She went on: "Everybody is trying to find their way, and has that fear, but use it and go with it. Don't look back and regret, give it a go, failure is fine. Just make sure whatever you're doing you don't risk the fundamentals of your life – stop when your risk is too much, eg your family, your home."

But, and here is the underlining of her Cojones mindset as she rightly and emphatically repeated, "Just don't let fear get in the way of success."

Very much like my other Cojones Icon Barry Hearn, she talked to me of calculated risk, but if fear is the only thing holding you back, then you'll only regret it if you don't have a crack.

I have given talks to large groups of women about the whole notion of Cojones, and it is interesting how many feel constrained by many of the age-old beliefs about a woman's role in society and the home, as well as the intimidation they feel in the business world.

Hats off to Sarah, who has simply demonstrated what a woman can indeed achieve with that Cojones mindset.

Ross Kemp - Cojones - Fullstop!

British and even American readers will likely know of Ross. He hit fame in the UK as one of the lead actors in the British soap *Eastenders*, where he played the hard man character Grant Mitchell.

After leaving *Eastenders* though, he became arguably more famous, and certainly more respected, when he embarked on documentaries in some of the most dangerous parts of the world with some of the most dangerous people.

In fact, with his hard man character in *Eastenders*, the coincidence was that he would go off and do some of the most daring TV work including *Ross Kemp on Gangs*, a documentary series exploring the impact of modern gang culture in the UK and around the world, *Ross Kemp in Afghanistan*, and *Ross Kemp: Extreme World*, amongst numerous others.

A true to life hard man you may say, certainly someone who is very brave and gutsy.

Now, I'm not advocating in any way that adopting the Cojones Code means going to the most unsafe parts of the world and shooting documentaries amongst violent gangs and tribes, but there are lessons we can learn from a man who has. Ross himself.

The first thing he mentioned, which makes sense really, was that they didn't just turn up in these crazy places and put themselves straight into the face of danger. A lot of planning goes into these investigative documentaries alongside intelligence experts who advise accordingly to control the risk exposed to.

The main reason he claimed he was able to have the courage to shoot documentaries in these extremely dangerous situations was the close knit team. The combined confidence. The team courage. He freely admitted that "If you are not scared of bullets passing over your head, then there is something wrong with you." So, the intense planning and the closeness of the team enabled that fear to be reduced dramatically.

I reminded him that in one of the programmes he did, two men had pointed rifles at him. I mentioned that instead of acting in total fear, he'd dealt with it with confidence, enabling him amazingly to defuse the situation. Poignantly, he then pointed out that like in any type of situation that has an element of danger, and confidence to deal with that, "If you hesitate when you go into a situation like that you are going to come off second best."

As someone who practises martial arts, I know that if you look like a scared weakling you are far more likely to attract a bully or a mugger than if you look like someone of confidence. So Ross's experience is proof of that, albeit on a far more extreme scale.

He admitted that when he was originally offered the opportunity to work on these dangerous documentaries he had no family of his own at the time, so thought less of the risks, but gave this final piece of important advice: "When an opportunity presents itself, you have to grab it with both hands, and be aware when that opportunity is presenting itself."

I found Ross to be very humble of his experiences, particularly as there are not many who'd take on such extreme dangers, but what came across strongly, and perhaps unsurprisingly, were the importance of teamwork (a problem shared is a problem halved) and thorough planning (as referred to by other icons earlier).

Chris Eubank - Cojones for Being Different and for Being Oneself

Here is a man who for those who don't know anything about boxing still know who he is.

Yes, he was a successful pro boxer winning world titles and making numerous defences of his belt, but he is perhaps most famous for his out of the ordinary, maverick dress sense and personality, hence his general celebrity status outside of the boxing world.

He's a man who has been mocked more than most for his outrageous dress sense, mockingly imitated by many for his distinctive voice that has a lisp, none more so than myself who actually phoned a sports radio show posing as Chris, and getting away with it. Funnily, the next day, a well-regarded boxing reporter wrote about Chris phoning this national radio show in a national newspaper. Only later did he find out it wasn't Chris, but it was me! Not only that, I even booked a table at a restaurant on Valentine's Day at the last minute whilst imitating and posing as him over the phone; the manager bent over backwards to accommodate me (well Chris actually) such was his status.

Here's a man who had a tough upbringing, and made good through his own tenacity and hard work to become a top professional boxer, something one can already admire. But what I, and perhaps many, should also admire and try to model is his ability to remain true to himself and his own uniqueness.

Most people, as we know from earlier in the book, try their absolute best to conform to what are deemed society's norms, going against their innate character, as we are taught from an early age the do's and don'ts of how to live as best we can with others in society. How fake. Chris is someone who is different and despite considerable mocking (including from myself as just seen) has remained true to his unique innate self. That takes Cojones, and he has them.

Whilst I am a big boxing fan, and admire Chris for the Cojones he showed as a professional athlete, I was most keen to interview him, which I did for the Cojones TV YouTube channel, for having the Cojones for being different, and indeed, for being himself at the same time.

Here are a few soundbites from my interview with him:

"Poverty was my nutrition."

"The less I had the more I wanted."

"I decided at 17 I was going to use that poverty as my motivation."

Inspiring words I would say, because if you are really motivated to do something big, the motivation will exceed the fear. It will propel you.

So, what is your motivation?

With regard to his personality and dress sense, here is what he said: "If you fit in, you will be like your peers. If you want to be extraordinary, you need to behave extraordin*arily.* You can't behave ordinary and expect to be exceptional."

"If you climb, make progress, it usually upsets people; if someone doesn't like the way you dress, it's not to do with you, it's to do with them."

"For every best dressed man award I won, I probably got laughed at 20 times."

"If you want to be successful be who you are."

"Others should be liberated by those who are not afraid to be themselves. When we let our own light shine we unconsciously allow others to do the same."

You have to say that as much as one may have laughed at him, which he admits, the words he came out with in my interview with him are amazingly inspirational, and should be to you. Listen to his words, heed them, follow them, and for sure you will be adopting the Cojones lifestyle.

So above you have some of the Cojones Icons I have interviewed to date whilst writing this book. There will be others subsequent to this, but let's just briefly take a look at some others that to my mind are worth including, but who I haven't spoken to, yet.

The Arsenal 1989 Championship Winning Team - Cojones to Defy The Odds

I simply had to take this example, not only because they are my football (soccer to my American readers) team, but because this particular team in the club's history, and manager at the time George Graham, had Cojones in abundance.

In those days there was one team in English football who dominated more than any team has in history here, Liverpool FC. The league title, which is considered the main yardstick of who is the best team, was won by Liverpool pretty much every season. No one ever gave any other team a chance, such was their utter dominance in the English game.

Arsenal at the time were managed by George Graham, who took over three years earlier, and whose aim was, indeed, to take Arsenal to the top, to challenge Liverpool's dominance, and break it.

That season Arsenal had a young team, and a team of winners, guided by Graham who proved himself to have that mindset, and he drilled that into his players. That season Arsenal were top of the league for long periods until the final two games of the season when it looked as if, with two games to go, the title again was going to Liverpool.

However, what was most bizarre was that the final game of the season (due to the game's postponement resulting from the Hillsborough tragedy) was Liverpool v Arsenal at Liverpool's home ground of Anfield, and for Arsenal to take the league title away from Liverpool they needed to win at Anfield by two clear goals: not even on goal difference but on goals scored.

No team ever went to Anfield and beat Liverpool, and certainly not by two goals, and certainly not to take their title, which had effectively belonged to them for what seemed like a lifetime. Arsenal did it, scoring the second goal in injury time to win 2-0, and win the league.

It was Arsenal that broke Liverpool's dominance. It was Arsenal, led by George Graham the manager, and the players who had the Cojones to do it, against all the odds. Again, the mindset and Cojones of this team is, if learned from, invaluable for all of us in our quest for results in our own life.

They went against the country's expectations of them to fail, and gallantly. They had a plan set by the manager, who instilled into them they **could** indeed do it, and they did, in what was one of the most amazing nights in football history.

Sacha Baron Cohen - Cojones to Have Fun

Again, sadly, I haven't interviewed him and would love to as not only do I enjoy his comedy, I admire his very ballsy approach.

One of the messages I like to relay to audiences is that having Cojones also entails finding out what moves you. Sorry to digress, but I love the film *School of Rock*, and one message I got from that film is that the one thing that allows the main character to express himself, and be who he is, is music. So have a think about this, what gets you going? How do you feel you can truly express yourself?

Now, one of the things I am known for is phone pranks. Childish maybe, but when I do it I entertain myself. It's like unlocking a code whereby the door of my innate self is opened wide.

Why am I referring to this? Because I think, although I can't say for sure as I am yet to speak to him, that Sacha, when he does the skits and interviews as one of his characters Ali G or Borat, he unlocks a code for himself that lets his talent flood out. I would say that helps his Cojones to stage some of his daring skits.

If you don't remember, to name a few, as his Kazakh character Borat he sang the American national anthem at a rodeo using altered lyrics that poked fun at the few thousand 'extreme' patriots in the Deep South of the US. It was hilarious, but perhaps a tad dangerous. Yet I'm sure that part of him was howling with laughter at what he was getting away with, and enjoying his Cojones moment.

Or when he sang an anti-Semitic song 'Throw the Jew Down the Well' to some, let's say less than refined, people, who joined in. Little did they know that Sacha was mocking them, as well as himself, as he is Jewish.

Again, to me it was hilarious. But the cheek and audacity he showed, which I am certain was entertaining for himself whilst doing it. A pure Cojones moment.

What can we learn from him? Find your own code for what allows you to be authentic, and 'in the zone', and the Cojones you may require to do it will likely come naturally to you.

Sylvester Stallone - Cojones to Keep Going

This man needs no introduction being one of the most successful film actors, writers, directors and producers, particularly with the success of his most famed characters Rocky and Rambo.

Stallone's major breakthrough was with his boxing character and story, Rocky. Stallone wrote the script in 20 hours, and subsequently attempted to sell the script to multiple studios, and received rejection after rejection after rejection after rejection.

Additionally, he was clear that he wanted to play the main role himself, making it harder to be successful, particularly as an unknown as he was at that time. Nevertheless, he never stopped going, and kept going and going and going.

Because of the intention of playing the lead role himself, Irwin Winkler and Robert Chartoff became interested and offered Stallone US$350,000 for the rights, but had their own casting ideas for the lead role, including Robert Redford and Burt Reynolds. Stallone refused to sell unless he played the lead character and eventually, after a substantial budget cut to compromise, it was agreed he could be the star. It ended up being a huge hit with umpteen sequels of course, and in turn made him one of the biggest film stars in the world.

He's a man I'd love to interview, to learn about his extraordinary tenacity and mindset that allowed him to keep going despite poverty and several knock-backs. One thing's for sure, he had a plan, he had a vision, he was relentless in his pursuit of his ultimate goal and never wavered from that.

Like pointing a magnifying glass using the sun's strength to hone in and burn paper, he had that same type of attitude to where he was going, and he is to me a Cojones Icon, and possibly my favourite.

Donald Trump - Cojones to Ride Criticism

I know exactly what you're thinking. How can you use him as someone to model or look up to in any way? I do get that. But please, please, hear me out for a minute. As I have discussed, you don't have to like someone per se to admire certain traits of theirs, and there are some things to admire about Donald Trump.

Really, you say? Yes, absolutely.

I have spoken with many people who despise Trump, but nearly all, when they stop to think about it in a neutral way, have a certain admiration for a few of his traits. I am talking more about him becoming president of the United States of America, rather than his business dealings and undoubted success. Although one does need balls to do what he has done in creating the business empire that he has, regardless of the fact that he was lucky enough to have had $10 million to start with.

Anyway, when I heard that he was putting himself forward as a candidate for the Republican nomination, my wife said to me, "Do you think he has got a chance?" to which I replied, "Do me a favour, no chance whatsoever." The truth is, most people would have said exactly the same thing, and many in the US did as well. But most importantly, did he listen to them? No chance.

He got the Republican nomination against all the odds. Subsequently, people thought he had no chance of becoming president. All the critics said he had no political experience, was totally unsuitable (many still say that), and simply didn't have the qualities to become president of the most powerful country on earth.

Again, did he listen? No. And he defied the odds against the tide. For that alone he does warrant some respect.

Most of us are put off doing far less, by our parents, guardians and peers. We are put off by our own 'doubting Tom' talk, let alone others'. He didn't, and had a target, then kept going until his target was reached. He is a man of serious Cojones. A man able to simply turn a deaf ear to all the doubters out there, a man who has belief in himself. And, as I mentioned already, Henry Ford said, "Whether you think you can, or you think you can't – you're right." How true this quote is in Donald J Trump's case.

OK, maybe he is pig ignorant, but don't you wish you could deflect criticism and doubters as easily as he does?

I have never, up to now, had the opportunity to interview him, and it is something I would very much like to do, but if I could learn and take his what seems to be unshakeable self-belief and tenacity, surely that is something worth having, isn't it?

Again, there may be traits that these come with that the detractors, including myself, would not want and I understand that, but hey, let's model what is and could be useful for us.

Margaret Thatcher - Cojones for Bloody-Mindedness

Here's another who needs little introduction, and one who is also either 'a love 'em or hate 'em' person. Regardless, she was Britain's first female and longest-serving prime minister.

Often a divisive character, which actually most people who stand for something often are, but an amazingly strong woman who came to prominence at a time when it really was a man's world, and a lot harder to make it to the top. Forgetting her gender for one second, you'll remember that she was considered so strong, so gutsy and so single-minded in how she thought her policies would be most successful for Britain, she was known as the 'Iron Lady'.

Of course, to be a man and to have held office as leader of Britain for the longest of anyone in the 20th century, and do it with utter steadfastness, and yes 'ballsiness', despite considerable divisiveness amongst the people, would be something remarkable, but to be a woman and do it is even more impressive.

Sadly, Margaret Thatcher died in 2013, so I'll never get the chance to interview her and learn more intimately what made her tick, and how she was so strong against the tide of adversity.

What it does show you is that if you can remain strongly and unbreakably attached to your principles, you will be living according to the Cojones Code, so study Maggie Thatcher for those traits, as for sure if you employ anything of her mindset it will hold you in good stead.

I could continue listing my Cojones Icons, but I'll likely do that in another book in its own right. What's important for now is thinking about who your own icons are, what traits they have that make them as such in your mind and how you can obtain some of their qualities.

We'll be looking more closely now at the qualities that make a Cojones Icon in the next chapter.

CHAPTER 10:

IDENTIFYING THE QUALITIES OF COJONES ICONS

So I've identified a few of my own Cojones Icons, including people I have interviewed for Cojones TV, and in doing so, after looking closely at them, I have been able to identify some of the actual qualities they have been able to harness in order to do what they do.

These qualities that I have identified allow a person to understand what is needed to adopt the Cojones Code into their lives. So what are they?

Focused

This one is obvious I know, but you can be sure that any of the Cojones Icons I have interviewed, or indeed anyone you may consider an icon, will have harnessed this essential tenet to achieve whatever it is they have done. The funny thing is, this can often be the hardest quality to adopt. They do say that discipline is the difference between what you want now and what you want! How true, but sometimes difficult to employ, considering all the distractions there are.

But what is it that you want? Whilst writing this book, snooker is on TV, so is football, so is tennis. I want to watch them *now*. But they aren't what I want in the long term. What I really want is to finish this book so you can feel it in your hands and enjoy, I hope. So, I have to remain focused.

To be honest, I would say this isn't so much a Cojones quality but a more general and necessary quality that goes hand in hand with any Cojones quality/behaviour I have identified or am about to. So, I'm not going to spend much more time on this one.

One thing I would say is whilst approaching anything that you want to achieve or desire to do, be focused, and if you want to adopt the Cojones mindset to do it, then be focused on harnessing the qualities of Cojones.

Conviction

Take Nigel Farage as an example. Now please, put your political aspersions to one side as this book is apolitical. Just look at the qualities he has and has needed to push his agenda forward and achieve what he wanted, which was ultimately to get the UK out of the EU, or at least ensure the prime minister gave the electorate a referendum.

The one thing that he had was absolute conviction is his beliefs. I asked Nigel when I interviewed him whether it was a totally selfless act, and he said without giving it any thought that it was. He had utter conviction that what he was doing was the right thing (certainly in his eyes) and was focused and driven to seeing it through no matter how long, how much energy, and how difficult the task. In fact, his conviction saw him through despite enormous criticism, confrontation and numerous detractors. He never wavered, and for that quality alone you have to take your hat off to him.

So yes, conviction is a quality of Cojones, and one that may be needed in the area of ballsy characteristics that you would be wise to adopt. It is perhaps a quality of Cojones that you can't learn, as you need to have passion about something that drives your conviction. There are things you could think about now, ie what are you passionate about? How passionate you are will affect how much conviction you have.

Now, Nigel has other Cojones qualities that enabled him to push forward his conviction, so this quality alone may not be enough on its own, so has to go hand in hand with others, focus being one of them.

But hey, if you have a strong conviction on something you want to change in the world, the wider world or indeed your own, then that is a great place to start, because if something is so important to you, you will do your utmost to harness the other Cojones qualities you need to see it through to fruition. Nigel Farage did.

Ride Criticism

I have already identified in the previous chapter how my Cojones Icons such as Alastair Campbell, Nigel Farage, Sylvester Stallone, and probably all of them have a wonderful ability to ride criticism, and this is a vital ingredient of Cojones. These people have had to endure some enormous levels of criticism (some deserved, you may say), and yet still kept going, and going, and going.

As a collector of quotes, as you will see at the end of the book, here's one that says a lot about this: 'You wouldn't care so much about what people think about you when you realise how seldom they do.' This saying is so true. Most of us find it hard when we receive criticism from others, to the extent of letting it put us off from doing whatever it is we are doing. But when you bear this quote in mind, should criticism really affect you? Should you really care what people think of you? **No.**

There are so many visionaries in the world and in history who were mocked, derided and criticised but had the conviction in what they were doing that they paid scant regard to the detractors, and carried on forward.

And yes, in the scheme of things people rarely think about you, or care about you in the way your feelings would have you believe, so why give their criticism any power? You shouldn't. And again, if you cared about something that much, and if you had relentless passion, you would care even less about people's harsh words or thoughts.

If you want to adopt the Cojones Code into your life, to get the results you crave, you simply have to be able to ride criticism. It goes with the territory of being different, or being yourself. If people don't like it, then tough. You have your life to lead, and as a dear friend of mine always tells me, if you don't get on the dance floor yourself, it's very easy to criticise someone else's dancing. If you are focused and passionate, then you won't let criticism deter you.

Anyhow, the obstacles of criticism are only in the way when you take your eyes off the target or goal. Focus on the goal and you'll barely see or hear the criticism. By the way, that also includes self-criticism, but I think if you go back and read earlier chapters where we talk in depth about thought, you should have enough knowledge to negate your own thoughts and talk. The same principle applies however, that if you are passionate about the target, and stay focused and put your energy there, your own ability to ride your own self-criticism will be strengthened.

Say It As It Is

Interestingly, and as you will already know from reading earlier chapters (at least, I hope you have), that this quality is effectively one of the Cojones Ten Commandments. And when you look at some of my Cojones Icons, they are not afraid to say it as it is.

Of course, this isn't a Cojones quality that is essential for whatever it is you want to do, although certainly befits examples such as David Walsh or Nigel Farage and the like, albeit in very different ways, because that is partly where their ballsiness lies.

Again, this quality tends to go hand in hand with the earlier qualities highlighted, because without being able to ride criticism you may not be so confident in saying it as it is, and maybe too, if you are not passionate about something you also may not say it as it is. So, like the commandments, this Cojones quality is only part of the jigsaw, but certainly allows you to be more authentic and true to your beliefs, and when you are, you will doubtless be more ballsy.

As I maintain, you can't be someone who says it as it is without having additional qualities of Cojones, but if you are confident enough in yourself, confident enough in what you believe and say, and you do say it, then purely by this practice you will become more ballsy overall.

Remember having Cojones is about being authentic, being yourself, not cow-towing to the so-called societal norms which may or may not be right, and embracing what it is about you that is unique and being proud of it, so start practising this part of authenticity.

Has A Go

People with Cojones all seem to have this essential quality, and as I said to you, often it is better to regret what you have done than what you haven't, and that means having a bloody go. It means you may have to do things that are outside your comfort zone, things you'd love to do, striving for things you want. Well you can't unless you have a go. A proper go.

The only failure in life is failure to try, although I must point out that simply 'trying' can indicate failure, because it's not about just trying. The word try actually indicates failure in a way. You can't *try* and give up smoking for example, you either do it or you don't. Many people I know said they tried giving up smoking for two months. They didn't give up then, did they?!

If I said to you, "Try and lift your arm," you'd lift your arm. You can't try really. You either do it or you don't! I am being a tad facetious, but just want you to get the point.

So, as one of my Cojones Icons Barry Hearn said, you have to take calculated risks if that's relevant to whatever it is you are 'trying' to achieve. In his own words though, he said, "If you do your homework, you'll pass the exam." OK, that's more of a business type of tip, but it makes sense,

All these qualities of Cojones are interlinked of course. If you have a go, but are not focused, or passionate, or can't ride criticism from yourself and others, you will likely not have a **good** go, and I mean have a bloody good go.

All of my own Cojones Icons, in whatever it is they have done, have always had a damned good go. If they don't succeed, then they'll all more than likely dust themselves off and have a damned good go at something else. But the notion of having a go in the Cojones sense relates largely with having no fear, and having a crack. These Cojones Icons will not have achieved anything if they didn't embrace this belief, or behaviour.

So, whatever it is you want to do – a business idea, political ambition, a sporting hobby, or asking a girl on a date, or chatting one up on the bus – throw more caution to the wind, and yes, as per one of the Cojones Ten Commandments, Like Nike, except 'FFS' Just Do It.

By the way, for women reading this book, I do apologise that I refer to men a lot in the romantic aspirational sense. By all means, reverse the role, except I'll be honest, I am a bit of a traditionalist and believe men should take the romantic initiative, but if you think differently, please don't be offended, and by all means also have a damned good go.

Play

If you can ride criticism, and have a go, whilst not basing your whole life's happiness or deemed success on it, and are able to simply have fun and play, imagine how easy adopting the Cojones Code may be.

Many of my Cojones Icons see what they have done or have set out to do as fun. Yes, it may be serious, but ultimately they have embraced the journey of getting there, and enjoy the fact that whilst they will do their best it may or may not turn out as they'd like it to, so they decide or decided to roll the dice and play.

It is this, it could be argued, that is at the heart of having or developing Cojones. By playing, you take things less seriously than you need to, meaning you are more relaxed — more relaxed at the outcome, more relaxed about what others and yourself say, meaning it's easier to ride criticism, easier to have a go, and whilst keeping the passion and focus, you are able to do things in an utterly relaxed way.

I chose as one of my Cojones Icons Sacha Baron Cohen, who as a comedian has done some of the most ballsy things in the name of entertainment. It may not be everyone's cup of tea, although a lot of it is mine I must say, but whilst I haven't to date interviewed him and got deeper as to what gives him his Cojones, one thing I am prepared to guess at, with an element of conviction, is that he's playing, having fun, and entertaining himself at the same time as entertaining others. I reckon that doing some of the ballsy things he does to get a laugh, he gets a big thrill seeing what he can get away with in the name of fun. He probably loves it, surprises himself, and possibly finds it rather liberating.

What do you find liberating? One of the reasons I like doing pranks (I know you probably find it a tad childish) is because I entertain myself, I'm playing, and yes, many things I do that others think take Cojones is just me playing.

So, this is an important quality of Cojones, and if you want to adopt the Cojones Code, then *play*. Have fun with whatever you are doing, as the heat, the fear you and others put on yourself, will be largely extinguished as a result. You will also be far more relaxed. Now, how much better are you at doing anything when you are relaxed? I know the answer, and I know you know the answer. So, go ahead and play.

Energy/Being A Force

I would say that all of the Cojones Icons that I have referred to have this quality. And when I say energy, I don't mean the energy you need to go for a workout, I'm talking about the drive you may be willing to put behind an idea, and putting force behind it.

It has some similarities to passion that I outlined earlier, but actually I'd go further and consider it to be a type of charisma that is noticeable. In fact, it's a drive that someone has that you can feel when you hear them speak, or when simply in their presence. It's an energy that surpasses passion, because it's a hard to grasp blend of immense passion and charisma. Being a force, I have identified, has to contain both of these.

How you get this quality we will explore further in the next chapter. However, if you do manage to adopt this quality, I would say with some confidence you have qualities that the average person does not – Cojones, that you apply to part of your life, or a context (a part of your life) that it relates to.

Chutzpah

Many people will not know this word. It is a Yiddish word for outrageous audacity, cheek and boldness.

For those who don't know, Yiddish is an old language spoken before the Second World War by Eastern European Jews. It was a mixture of German and Hebrew, with many words finding their way into our own English language, and few words sum up a quality of Cojones better than chutzpah.

It is a huge part of the Cojones way of life. In actual fact, when you look at the Jewish community, estimated in the world to be 0.25% of the world's population, they are very successful in comparison to their numbers, be that in science, business, hi-tech, entertainment etc. There are a few reasons for that: hard work, the insistence on study from an early age, but I would say chutzpah plays a massive part, and part of that being 'if you don't ask you don't get'.

When I interviewed TV barrister Judge Rinder, himself Jewish, he said he was wondering how one could define chutzpah, and said, "The ultimate chutzpah is murdering your parents then claiming the family estate." OK, rather extreme you may say, or very extreme actually, but tongue in cheek and a wonderfully funny analogy of the word, at how being audacious, bold and perhaps fearless, all part of the Cojones mindset, can bolster your quest for success in whatever it is.

Judge Rinder will have used his own chutzpah to get himself from successful barrister to hugely popular TV barrister and celebrity. How? Well, he had the audacity, drive and fearlessness to push his scripts to producers, and when he met that one person who liked what he did, he followed it up, before finally the doors to his TV success began to open.

In my eyes, chutzpah perhaps more than anything means having a real edge in anything you embark upon. It is having front, being cheeky, and ultimately doing stuff where you don't give too much of a damn about the outcome, as well as who you offend in the process. It sounds dramatic in a sense for all those who daren't do this or that, nor say this or that.

Chutzpah, sadly, is to my mind the hardest quality to model and adopt. Why? Because much depends on your personality, a natural innate cheekiness to pull it off. As we'll see later, and as mentioned above, not giving a damn about the process nor the outcome will help you enormously.

Adhering pretty religiously to some of the relevant Ten Commandments will go some way to giving you some chutzpah.

Luck, one says, is the meeting of preparation and opportunity, and chutzpah, which is essential outrageous audacity, will undoubtedly ensure you have more opportunities, as well as enabling you to take advantage of them. A key component of Cojones.

So, I've identified some of my own Cojones Icons, and in this chapter looked at some of the qualities they have demonstrated that have allowed them to achieve in their particular field. You of course will have your own idea of who your Cojones Icons are, so go ahead and identify yours. Then perhaps you can further identify the qualities they have that has given them Cojones.

In the next chapter we'll take a look at some ways we can model these icons and their qualities, and how we can go some way to adopting these for ourselves and our own life.

CHAPTER 11:

MODELLING ICONS

So I've identified some of my own icons and broken down what factors have largely contributed to the success they've had in their particular area. But how can we model them?

Neuro-Linguistic Programming (NLP), a subject we touched on in Chapter 4, is, according to some of its exponents, most relevant in the Study of Excellence. This includes taking a model of something, someone, or an organisation and breaking down into great detail the strategies and workings of that model, so as to be able to employ those same strategies and mode in order to obtain similar results in whatever it is you are trying to achieve.

This further involves, in the case of a person, breaking down his strategy in terms of when and how he uses the five senses (Visual,

Auditory, Kinaesthetic, Olfactory and Gustatory), and modelling that strategy.

Whilst this is a valuable approach, I believe it is somewhat unrealistic, and not always feasible, as one would really need to spend time with the subject to obtain the fine detail required in the NLP theory of modelling. Do you have the time and energy to do that? Probably not.

To apply it is also to my mind not so easy, so we will try and simplify things somewhat. By doing so, we will hopefully be able to embrace, learn and utilise certain qualities more easily in order to adopt the Cojones Code for your own life and/or particular context for what you are trying to attain or obtain.

The important thing to know is that, as always, it's action that counts more than thought. So when you look at modelling any Cojones Icon after having identified his or her traits, you must relate it to taking action – *not* thought.

Motivation

The first thing to help you model anyone is to find out what motivates them.

As we've seen in the last chapters, each Cojones Icon has a different motivator, a different catalyst to their ballsiness. I accept that unless you have a chance to interview or speak at length with someone it's not always so easy to identify the workings of their inner mind.

But you don't have to model a Cojones icon who is well known or famous. You may have friends or acquaintances whose ballsy qualities you'd like to have a bit of. If you have, then meet with them, tell them you admire them, and then, with their permission, ask them some questions that could help you learn from them. Most people would not have an issue with that, and actually would be most complimented that you or anyone would want to learn from them because they are admired.

Now of course you can check out my *Cojones Icons* series on Cojones TV on YouTube to get an idea of the questions I asked to obtain some insight into the workings of their mind. Having said that, it should be a whole lot easier if it's someone you know, because they'll likely be easier to pin down and get more time from. Because my highlighted ones are 'celebrities' of a sort, their time is harder to get a piece of.

Also, the type of question you ask can depend on the kind of person you are looking to model, be that a businessman, a sportsman, a politician or anyone.

But here are a few types of questions to pose:

What is/was most important to you in doing...?

How important is/was the cause for you?

Why was it that important to you?

What negative self-talk did you have?

How did you overcome that?

Are you ballsy in other areas of life?

When are you the opposite?

Are you utterly confident in your ability to...?

How did you muster the motivation to do...?

Have your fears hindered you, and how?

Have your fears driven you, and how?

Are/were you driven by your fear of failure? Or by desire for success? Can you explain?

Who are your Cojones Icons?

Is there one piece of advice from your life's experience and success that you could relate to myself and others?

Is your success and mindset down to a product of environment?

What were some moments that you look back on and thought that took real guts, chutzpah, and I can't believe I did that? How did you?

What kind of thoughts do you/did you have to go through before making that kind of decision?

Do you consider yourself particularly brave or courageous?

Can you elaborate on some of the very hard decisions you've had to make?

You must have been affected by stress and worry – how did you deal with it?

What makes you extraordinary and how would you advise the ordinary person how they can be like you?

When you were really up against it how were you able to ride that storm, financially or indeed mentally?

Was it something you used as fuel to burn in your quest for success?

These questions and more will give you useful information that will enable you to learn and model from your Cojones Icons.

Focused

As per our identification of qualities of Cojones Icons in Chapter 9, *focused* is another essential quality they all have demonstrated. When you think of it, being focused is actually a by-product of motivation, so if you have identified the motivator for yourself, you will likely be a lot more focused on what it is you are trying to achieve.

If you are modelling an icon to enhance your own Cojones, then you will as above notice that every icon has a motivator. What are yours? What would success be for you? Why do you want it?

Success is a very ambiguous word, as everyone has a different yardstick for success. Many would say success is measured by power, wealth, number of children, happy marriage, good health, but here, for the purpose of adopting Cojones, it has to be something that requires some balls, some boldness, some audacity.

Now, because we are all individual, and each of us has different levels of Cojones in different contexts, I want to ask you have you ever been focused? When was that? Silly question really, because we all have at some point in our lives. So what was it you were focused on? When was that?

Unlike a lot of self-help books, I'm not going to ask you to make a list, although you can if you want. But here's the thing, if you have been focused, what was it on? What was your motivation? Because motivation and caring enough go hand in hand. If you care enough, you'll be focused enough. Remember, discipline is the difference between what you want now and what you want.

So, look at the times you have been focused. Once you can identify them you can at least know you are capable of being so. Then, identify the reasons why you were so focused. What were their drivers? Once you can get to the bottom of what the drivers were, you will know whether you can replicate it, and whether the motivation is there.

Now, today, is there something, or are there some things in which you need to be more ballsy to achieve?

By the way, if you want to be a more ballsy person generally, then you will need to practise this in a number of contexts. But once you can identify times where you've been focused, and know why, how, and where (yes, environment can change your mindset as we will see later), you can then start to reproduce it in other areas of your life.

Conviction

What are you passionate about? On what do you have strong convictions? Do you express them? What would happen if you did? What would happen if you didn't?

Sorry if I am sounding a tad repetitive, but can you see there is a pattern that forms with this exercise? Because if you really have conviction about something, yes you will be more focused, yes you will be more motivated, and yes you will be more ballsy, because the importance to you of it will override any of the inhibitions you may have, or at least it will help push you in that direction.

For example, do you believe utterly that you deserve a rise in wages, or would you simply like one?

Or, do you believe utterly that you have what it takes (backed up by research – your homework – as one of my Cojones Icons, Barry Hearn, would say) to make a success of your business idea?

Or, do you believe completely that you deserve to be treated with respect?

Or, do you believe fully that whatever it is you want to do you have what it takes to execute?

If so, then your conviction, which is indeed one of the qualities of Cojones Icons, will go some way to ensuring you are ballsy enough to carry it through.

Ride Criticism

Are you scared of criticism? From others? From yourself? Remember, you wouldn't be so bothered about what people think of you when you realise how seldom they do. As I said, all these qualities are intertwined, but often being able to ride criticism, assuming you are motivated, focused and have conviction in whatever it is.

Bear in mind, if you are aiming to do something with an edge, that's a little bit different, then naturally, you will be shot down in flames. It goes with the territory. People love to mock and put down anyone who's a bit different, or able to try something different as we have already learned. So learning from a Cojones Icon means you will have to learn to ride criticism.

Again, if you satisfy the first qualities of focus, motivation and conviction, you will be more likely to develop the bull in a china shop behaviour, and literally ride the criticism naturally as you won't have the time nor the mental energy to be bothered by it.

If what people say is more important to you than your catalyst/motivator in what you are trying to achieve, then you don't satisfy the first three qualities above on what could be titled the Cojones Qualities Ladder. This means you will not be able to achieve what you want to, as you haven't adopted the Cojones Code... yet.

Now I know, some people are more sensitive than others, and much depends on the level of criticism, but hey, Cojones is about being different, rising up, and making a difference in your life, and likely other people's too.

Have you ever seen the amazing musical with Hugh Jackman, *The Greatest Showman*, an amazing story about PT Barnum? One thing though that sticks in my mind among the many wonderful poignant moments in the film was when Hugh Jackman's character uttered these words: "No one ever made a difference by being like everyone else." How true, and how relevant in the case of living by the Cojones Code, and being able to ride criticism. Because people who make a difference, and aren't like everyone else, are more often than not mocked and criticised.

So if you want to make a difference, and be different, then you'll need to get used to taking some criticism. Remember though, most of the time, the critics are those who are jealous because they don't have your level of Cojones, boldness and audacity to do something different.

Oh, what about your own self-criticism you ask? Well we have covered this in chapters on CBT and the NLP meta model, so all I have to add to that is that most of the time your own self-criticism has been adopted because of the experience of criticism of others previously, and how you've believed their messages, more often than not, are lies.

Say It As It Is – When have you spoken your mind? Why? What was it about that situation that made you do so? Regardless, it proves you can, true? Why not replicate it?

Whilst this Cojones tenet isn't on a ladder specifically, it is an important aspect of living what I call the authentic Cojones lifestyle, because after all, it forms significant aspects of the Cojones Ten Commandments.

Now, I know, you may well hate some of the Cojones Icons that I've identified, particularly the somewhat divisive characters such as Nigel Farage, but hey, there are many, and you can identify your own. And sometimes one needs very strong examples to convey a message.

Just because they are outspoken does not mean that everyone who is outspoken like them is as divisive. Being outspoken can mean a number of things, from speaking out against what is morally right, asking for what you want from someone, demanding proper service from a company in which you are a customer or client, or simply standing up for your own self-respect. And again, whilst you may not like the people I've highlighted, you can still learn from them.

So, how can we model a Farage for example, in saying it as it is? Two things stand out as being part of this: being motivated and having conviction. Of course, if you haven't got these you are going to struggle to open your mouth if it's simply not worth it to you.

So in any situation, if needed, ask yourself what really matters to me? Or, does it really matter to me? If, and once you have responded with an emphatic yes, and bear in mind it **must** be an emphatic one, you have then set yourself up to doing something, in this case opening your mouth!

Here's another thing worth considering at the same time: do you like living in a world of tight-lipped bullshit? Sorry for the language, but if you want to live an authentic life, a quality of living via the Cojones Code, then you, like me, have no time for bullshit, and certainly not bullshitters, but sadly they are all around us.

Remember, adopting the Cojones Code is about not falling into the societal trap of pleasing everyone for the sake of it. If you have something to say, and it really matters to you, then you are a valid and valuable part of this world, so you have to say it, because what you say is important.

Imagine what the world would be like if everyone could just be open and honest, albeit in a diplomatic way. Refreshing eh? Sadly, the world seems to be going in the opposite direction to this right now. Well, you can't change the world, you can only change yourself.

So, back to how. Firstly, as I mentioned, care. Yes, if you care about something, if you have conviction and are motivated, then this is the first step to compelling you to take action.

Now, when have you 'said it as it is' before? I guarantee you have at some point opened your mouth before about something important. What was it? When was it? What pushed you to say whatever it was you needed to? What were your thoughts at the time? What did you feel at the time? Going further we could ask, what could you see at the time? What could you hear? Can you revisit the passion you were experiencing at that time?

In fact, you can literally revisit moments you have been able to do something, and by re-enacting it in your mind's eye, you will be preparing yourself and your neural pathways for action, because once you are in the right state, you will be of the right mindset to speak out.

It's interesting. Like most of this stuff, by practising this lifestyle you will do it more naturally. So perhaps start off with lesser risk scenarios. Less risk meaning where what you say will not be so beaten down, or even offensive to people. Less risk in which you don't feel as worried to open your mouth. Not that you should be, as you know by now.

Where could that be? How about phoning a radio show and voicing your opinions? How about going to discussion groups and getting stuck in? How about chatting with the people you are most comfortable with and start saying what you really want? Stuff that they don't care much about but allows you to build the 'speaking out' muscle. The more you practise, and I know it's a little obvious, the easier it will become.

Have A Go – This again has a number of different facets and qualities, because of the range of small and large things it could cover. But then, so what? Here's a quote I've already mentioned but it sums it up for me:

"Twenty years from now you will be more disappointed by the things you didn't do than by the things you did." Mark Twain

Just this wise quote alone could be enough to ignite you into action, because I am absolutely sure there will be times in your life, maybe not as many as in mine, but many times in which you have kicked yourself for not having a bloody go.

Go on, tell me I'm wrong! It's no good having regrets as such, but we all do it, and who needs self-bemoaning?

Now sometimes, you really don't need to think too much about having a go, because the risk to you could be minimal, and if so, what's stopping you?

When I was a hot-blooded young guy, I used to have numerous fears about asking a girl out, or chatting to them. But what was the risk? There really was none.

Stepping up to the plate in lower risk scenarios again will help you build the 'have a go' muscle, like the one I've just highlighted, and will build your Cojones I can tell you.

Of course, having a go examples which have financial, personal or health risks need to be assessed for their calculated risk first.

If you check out my interview with legendary British sports promoter Barry Hearn, when I asked him about his own Cojones, he said that anyone who has an idea who doesn't have a go is merely a dreamer. But he said his ideas have always undergone considerable research into their viability before deciding definitively whether to put them into action. As I have mentioned previously, he uses this analogy: "If you do your homework, you'll pass the exam."

So, if you are about to have a go, and it carries a genuine risk to your health, your finances, or even your marriage and personal life, then of course, you need to weigh up the opportunity/cost. Another icon of mine, *Dragons' Den* Sarah Willingham, expressed that.

The higher the risk whatever it is, the greater the intelligent and informed research that's required, so I am not going to argue with Barry. He's right.

So, for all 'have a go' scenarios, I want you to ask yourself when have you thrown caution to the wind? Had a go? Not bothered about the outcome? How did it feel? What was the outcome? What was at stake? What was it that was different from any other situation? Can you replicate the parts of you that did that?

I want you to delve deep into your life experiences and research internally when you had a go. What was the risk? What were you thinking? What could you see? What could you hear? What could you feel?

I can tell you, one thing that's important in this quality of a Cojones Icon that I have identified through my talking to a number of them is what they're feeling before embarking on something. Often, they experience a tinge of excitement in their body, a physiological reaction that tells them 'I really want to do this' and it pushes them into action.

So I think the feeling aspect (or kinaesthetic as it is called) is the foundation of this Cojones quality, what feelings, what physiological responses did you have when thinking about doing whatever you planned? Did you have within you that tinge of excitement, that desire that expressed itself within you in the form of a physiological response? If so, then you'll want to replicate that to push on and do something.

This tinge is often not only the catalyst, but also the guide that tells you 'this is really important to me'. And of course, if it really is important to you, then you will have (or bloody well should have) the conviction, motivation and the focus **to do it.**

Energy/Being A Force

Can you get more animated? What gets you animated? What gets you excited? What enables you to be up for something? Again, can you replicate that?

Please forgive me for being repetitive, but it's all hugely relevant. All these traits have similarities and work together, ie often you can't have one without the other. But hey, look at my Cojones Icons, they all have an energy and are a force.

Now you may feel it could be described as one of the traits above, but take Nigel Farage as an example. Whether you love him or hate him, he's a force, he has a certain energy. Perhaps charisma, but I put it down to his conviction, focus, motivation etc.

You could say that conviction + focus + motivation = being a force.

I mentioned a type of Cojones Ladder, and yes, I do consider the components of the above equation to be perhaps the foundational qualities of any Cojones Icon. Now Nigel Farage, or any icon, will unlikely be that force in every aspect of life. It just so happens when you engage him on his passion, Brexit, he becomes an energy, a force.

Whatever you want to do, you need to embrace this. By harnessing the qualities mentioned you will naturally become a force, and here's the thing, by taking action with Cojones you will in any case become a force.

Chutzpah

To repeat, chutzpah is the Yiddish word meaning outrageous audacity.

I'll refer again to one of my Cojones Icons interviews with Judge Rinder, the UK's version of Judge Judy and his funny analogous definition of chutzpah being "murdering your parents and then claiming the family estate!" A black humour approach to defining this word, but in the right environment, or right scenario of course, one can do amazing things. Take a look at a few of these examples of chutzpah.

UK talent agent Jonathan Shalit, to remind you, wanted a job as a youngster and knew where the boss's office was of the company that he wanted to work for. He gave his CV to the window cleaner to put it on his desk and he ended up getting the job. That's chutzpah, and yes, a Cojones moment.

Now, I've had many. One of my favourites is the story I related earlier, in Chapter 3, about my time in telesales. To get through to the boss of a company in Cyprus who wouldn't take my calls, I put on my best Greek Cypriot voice, announced myself as George Polycarpou, and he took my call straight away! I pitched the deal and got the business.

Nice bit of chutzpah eh? And it is 100% true.

So, now you get an idea what chutzpah is. I'd say it's an important quality and fits nicely with many of the Cojones Ten Commandments.

So, tell me, ever thought to yourself 'I can't believe I did that? I can't believe I said that? How did I manage that?' If so, you most likely will have shown chutzpah before, so there's no reason why you can't recreate it.

In fact, have you ever done anything and wondered 'how the hell did I manage that?' Of course you have, and you know what? The more you think about it, remember it in detail, you can start to ask yourself many of the questions we have posed earlier in this chapter. What was I thinking at the time? What was my motivation? What was different in that situation from another? Once you know this, you will understand what it was in the past that has driven you to use chutzpah, and to having that real Cojones moment.

You may well have asked yourself 'What have I got to lose? What's the worst that can happen?' Perhaps the most important questions to ask yourself to push you to do something. In fact, go and write those questions down now, and keep asking yourself, because if I could sum up Cojones in two lines for action it would be these two questions.

Anyway, whilst I have pinpointed that chutzpah is one of the qualities of Cojones Icons, having Cojones is also a part of having chutzpah, they really do go hand in hand.

There is one thing which is harder to teach. That is that chutzpah is sometimes something triggered by a lightbulb moment of inspiration. That's exactly right, often merely an idea that sounds crazy, but hey, worth a try, like me being a Cypriot or Jonathan Shalit getting the window cleaner to put his CV on his future boss's table.

And this points back to another of the Cojones Ten Commandments: Don't Rip Up the Rule Book - Burn It Instead. So if you get a crazy idea that's worth a try and the risk (financial and health) is minimal, then what the hell – have a go. Use some chutzpah.

Play

What is mundane everyday that you could play at? What have you done, or do in your life that felt/feels light?

Here's an interesting question. What makes anything so important? If you said 'Fxxk it' and just did something for the challenge, for the fun, how would that be for you?

You know, this year I took my young son skiing for the first time. OK, he was lucky enough to have some private lessons which is a faster track to learning, but he had just three, two-hour lessons, and he was coming down a blue run with me after only three days.

OK, maybe he's a natural (I would say that, I am his dad), but he had no fear, it was simply **fun.** His aim was to have **fun.** Of course, had he had fear, for sure it would have impacted his ability to have fun, and as a result, his ability to progress as quickly as he did.

Of course, when we grow up, we get serious, and almost about everything. Why?

I know, I know, I've talked about it before, societal and parental infringements, and the over worry of risks. Then later on in life, the need to contribute to society, to get married, have 2.2 children, have a mortgage etc etc removes all our ability to have any fun, to enjoy life.

Here's another quote: "The tragedy of life is not that it ends so soon, but that we wait so long to begin it." W. M. Lewis

Seeing that life is so fragile, and so unpredictable, shouldn't we be doing our best to enjoy every moment as much as we can and have fun, loads of it? Of course the answer as Simon Cowell would say is "A big fat yes."

Now, of course, there's no doubt that any Cojones Icon I have referred to will have recounted the many days in his or her endeavours that were not fun at all, but in my studies of Cojones Icons I am sure that this quality, and the way an icon paints his or her picture, will tell you that whilst having tough times, they also had a lot of fun, and in many situations simply played, and enjoyed the 'game' or the chase.

This quality, whilst perhaps not as important as the others, is to my mind still vital.

If you could go into anything with the idea that you are going to play and have fun, then you will, in TA (Transactional Analysis) terms, be freeing up your free child, and like my son in skiing, be able to do things with far greater ease.

Has my young son got Cojones? Perhaps, but really, he just wants to play and have fun. Why when we are grown up do we lose that? Do you think you could play, or at least have fun in whatever you set out to do? You better start – *now.*

What about practising having fun in your current everyday work? Why not try being at work with more reckless abandon, in which you play more? I don't mean not doing the job, but treating it as a challenge, find out what makes you feel rewarded (not financial), and go for it.

Yes, this book is about having Cojones, but if you start applying and therefore practising the qualities of Cojones Icons, then you will be adopting the Cojones Code. You will become more ballsy, live a more authentic life by implication, and when you really want to go for something outlandish you will have exercised the Cojones muscle, and have a far greater chance of **doing** it, and as a result, a far greater chance of succeeding.

CHAPTER 12:

YOUR HISTORY OF LEARNING LIMITATION

Cast your mind back 50 years. I say that because I'm almost that age unfortunately. Crikey, where has time flown?

OK, if you can't, and I can't as I wasn't even born yet, but let's look back to when you were say ten years old. Do you remember what that was like? Do you remember the cars people drove, the phones people used, the radios we listened to? The world has evolved and become more advanced, and many of the things we thought were unimaginable are now a reality.

Why? Because it is natural for us to better ourselves, expand our comfort zones, seek improvement and achievement. I've mentioned it earlier, but without Cojones none of the things we take for granted today would be possible.

That's right. Cojones is the foundational catalyst for this evolution. Not, by the way, as many utopian gurus will say, "All you need to do is think it and it will appear."

So, if we go back 50 years, 100 years, 150, or even more, and we could tell the people who were living then the kinds of things we have now, the things we have got used to, they'd have said you were mad, or were just dreaming.

The paradox though is that if you ask most people, they are all so full of doubt about what is possible. Most people don't dare to dream. Most people don't believe in the impossible. But despite that, all these amazing advances and achievements have taken place. Why? Due to those people who don't believe in limits. Oh, and yes, Cojones.

Can you imagine how amazing the world would be if doubt and limitation was the rarity? How much further forward could we be? The possibilities are absolutely unimaginable and endless. When you consider what's been achieved in a world of, in general, only believing in the possible, a world where learning limitation is embedded into our belief system from a young age, you surely get a strong idea of what truly could be, if you believed in the impossible.

And I'm not only talking technology here, but who'd have thought 100 years ago that:

- There'd be a female prime minister – we've now had two

- A man could run 100 metres in 10 seconds or less

- Couples who couldn't conceive can have children via IVF

- Short-sightedness can be corrected via a laser beam (I had the procedure – amazing)

- You can get from London to Paris on a train in two hours

- You can have the worst sense of direction, yet never get lost with a GPS

- A building can be built over half a mile tall

- A black man would be the president of the United States of America

- A Muslim would be the mayor of London

- Gay people can marry and have children

These are literally a few that immediately spring to my mind, but the list is endless, and is continuing as we speak as boundaries get pushed out and achievements are made because there are a minority of people who believe that they **can.**

So, I'll ask it again, can you imagine how many more achievements there would have been, or could be, if we all had this mindset of 'what is possible', or perhaps even more pertinently that 'nothing is impossible'? When you look at it closer, the word impossible says I'm possible. This is framed and hung in the passageway of my young boy's school. Now that's what our kids need to be taught.

So where do we get the mindset of limitation? I have briefly touched upon it, but for the purpose of seeing how erroneous our way of learning is, I'll say it again, we learn it from our parents, guardians, peers and the media.

Like every organism, the programmed code for life is survival and reproduction. It's really our modus operandi. We are built that way, as is every living thing. But as human beings we are lucky enough to have the greatest power, that of cognition, followed by invention and betterment. We are aware that we have choices. But somewhere along the line we learn to limit them. We learn limitation.

I mentioned earlier that growing up I was of the belief that I wasn't clever. I wanted to be a vet when I was a kid, such was, and is, my love of animals. But my aunt and mum used to say, "Oh I think you have to be very clever to be a vet." Sadly, I understood that or took on the perception of I'm not clever enough. Many would have also, but then there are those who wouldn't have and ended up being vets anyway, in the same situation.

Of course, I could have turned round to them or even myself and contested "actually I am very clever", but I stupidly took it as a message that I was, indeed, limited. Nowadays of course, I would have taken the alternative stance as I know better, but when you think we all have some sort of dream of what our adult life will be like, rarely does it turn out that way.

I make it sound like my family were nasty or bad, but that's not the case at all, it's just the message they probably grew up learning, and as we are a product of the product it all stands to reason.

So nowadays I would stick the proverbial two fingers up at anyone who tries to transmit their own limiting beliefs on me, and you should do the same, because all the people I've referred to in this book will have embraced the possible, rather than the perception of the impossible. By the way, it is normally only a perception.

Have you ever been put off a dream or desire of your own by another person, be that family or friend? Or, do you walk around with latent dreams and desires, but been put off by the learned voices of negativity in your head?

Recently, I realised a 35-year-old dream. I bought myself a Golden Retriever puppy. Doesn't seem like much of a dream to some, but ever since my parents gave away my Golden Retriever when I was a kid, I have yearned for one. Now, only a week before picking him up, family members seemed intent on putting me off, saying, "It's too hard", "It's too much responsibility", "You shouldn't be getting one as you won't be able to manage it." First of all, it was none of their goddamn business, but provides a classic example of people intent on passing their own negativity and belief in limitation on to others.

And that was only about getting a puppy, something people do every day, but it was a dream of mine, and if I'd listened to them I wouldn't have fulfilled one of my own personal long-held wishes.

You see, the limitation they like to transfer on to us is really an expression of their own. So, leave them to deal with theirs. You must not let them pass it on to you. It's their problem, not yours, I promise you. I advise you to do what I did. Not listen to them, and actually say to yourself 'Fxxk 'em'. If you want to do something that will fulfil your dreams and wishes, then you do it, and don't let anyone tell you that you can't.

Remember again what Einstein said, "Great spirits have often encountered violent opposition from mediocre minds."

This is another lovely quote, I am a collector of them as you will see later, and whilst I am not necessarily saying all the naysayers have mediocre minds, what I do believe is that the quote expresses plainly that their minds are mediocre because they have allowed themselves to be mediocre, largely through their own frustration, and they want to impose that on others.

Well guys, this book is about adopting the Cojones Code, about growing a pair, and one step to doing so is not listening to those who through their own frustration want you to fail. And believe me, there *are* those who actually want you to fail, as you succeeding would only allow them to feel even worse about themselves and their own lack of balls and success, or at least having a good crack.

In fact, to go deep into the Cojones Code goes even further than that. It's not just about telling the naysayers to mind their own business, or worse, it's actually in putting around yourself people who will support your endeavours and encourage you. I advise you strongly to do that. Don't bother hanging around any type of toxicity.

At the same time, I'm not saying you should cut the enemies of your dreams totally out of your life. Well, I am really, although I accept that's not possible if they're family, but for sure, it makes sense to put 'can do-ers' around you. That's right, your Cojones environment.

I'm going to go deeper into this in the next chapter, where I touch on another NLP theory or practice known as the Logical Levels. So, read on.

CHAPTER 13:

THE LOGICAL LEVELS

Yes, here I go again, referring to a coaching theory.

I'll say it again, I am critical of many so-called life coaches, or people who have done brief courses in life coaching and then immediately think they can address the ills of someone's psyche. Actually, sometimes that's dangerous, but I do think in the context of my subject, Cojones, many coaching interventions and methods can help understand the notion whilst expediting growing a pair.

In addition, in the context of what I finished on in the last chapter, on who you put around you, your environment, I thought it pertinent to dedicate a chapter to the Logical Levels.

The Logical Levels are often defined as five levels of thinking or situation: identity, beliefs and values, capability or competence, behaviour and environment. They are usually visualised as a hierarchy. The basic idea behind the Logical Levels is that each level directly affects others in the hierarchy.

So, what are they?

In answering this, I will refer to what I learned when I studied NLP under the well-known Ian McDermott, which is, look at the following sentence:

I CAN'T DO THAT HERE

Only five words long, but powerful in five different ways. How? Try repeating it five times, each with the emphasis on a different word in the sentence, like this:

Statement 1 - **I** CAN'T DO THAT HERE

Statement 2 - I **CAN'T** DO THAT HERE

Statement 3 - I CAN'T **DO** THAT HERE

Statement 4 - I CAN'T DO **THAT** HERE

Statement 5 - I CAN'T DO THAT **HERE**

Now, go on, do it again, go through each of the above statements placing particular emphasis on the word in bold. How different does each sentence sound? Very different eh?

Same words, but different emphasis, and a wholly different meaning. First of all, it shows you how powerful words are when they are communicated in a different way, but what does each statement mean when they are said with those different emphases?

Statement 1 - This one refers to your Identity.

Or I mean to say, your own (or even others') perception of your identity. You may ask yourself who am **I** to do that? That's not **me**.

Now if you want to do anything, and you have some sort of deep belief about your identity, it limits your ability to go forward and **do** whatever it is you want to do. Therefore, you need to look into your own perceptions of your own identity, or even your requirement to take on other people's perception of what your identity should be.

This is important, because to apply any of the Cojones Commandments, and live the authentic Cojones way of life, it may well be infringed by issues you have within the first Logical Level surrounding identity.

Now, I'm not going to go into some therapy session, but what may be helpful in 'blockages' if you like, in all of the Logical Levels, is by applying questions we looked at in Chapter 4, when we looked at the NLP meta model and the CBT model of rationalising erroneous beliefs. I will recap at the end of this chapter though.

Statement 2 - This one refers to Beliefs and Values.

This is such a big one for so many, and a lot of it is relevant to what we discussed in the previous chapter about learning limitation. Well, we all learn limitation via our beliefs. And our beliefs are adopted largely through the learned messages and behaviours of our closest when we're growing up. But remember, underneath all these beliefs are simply thoughts, and again, in the chapter when we looked at the Three Principles, and looked at the power of thought, or the power we give it, we can see how erroneous our beliefs are.

When your thoughts are wholly different, you won't think about your identity in a restrictive way, and when you realise the power of thoughts, and how we don't need to take them seriously, leading to a belief change, your decision about your ability to **do** will also change. The perceived impossible becomes possible, or 'I'm possible'.

Statement 3 - This one refers to Capability. The how!

Now here I'd like to requote again one of my Cojones Icons, and actually my favourite, sports promoter Barry Hearn, who said to me, "If you do your homework, you'll pass the exam."

What more do I really need to say, except if you are to embark on anything, then do your bloody homework? I sound like a parent or schoolteacher, but whether you are starting a business, preparing for a sports tournament, auditioning for a part, then prepare.

Failing to prepare is preparing to fail, and if you don't put in the donkey work, the prep, then you by nature will be less brave, more fearful, or at least you should be. And if you are not, then perhaps you are too cocky.

Cojones is about having no fear, but if you don't put in the effort to be **able**, to be cap**able**, then you don't really deserve to achieve the results you want.

Now, I did say that the thing with the Logical Levels is that each level directly affects others in the hierarchy. So, if you haven't got the capability, then by rights you should be lower in the beliefs department. If you are low on belief that you can attain the capability, then it will naturally be harder to achieve the capability, etc etc, and round and round it goes.

But, as the oldest adage says, 'Practice makes perfect', and what that means is pull your finger out or as Mr Hearn says, "Do your homework."

Statement 4 – Behaviour.

Did I mention the notion of 'Act as If?' or 'Fake it to Make it'?

Did you know, your physiology affects your psychology and vice versa? It does.

Take a sad person. What does their physiology look like? Probably shoulders slumped, eyes looking downwards. What happens if the sad person changes his or her physiology to shoulders being upright, chest out, looking straight ahead or more upwards? I will answer that for you: their psychology changes.

This works both ways. As Malcolm Gladwell wrote in his book *Blink*, just doing the action of smiling brings about changes to your psychological state. If you are in a good mood your physiology will reflect that. So when we talk about behaviour, I am a strong advocate of the concepts of 'Act as If' and 'Fake it to Make it' as on their own they are very powerful tools to know about and employ.

I know many NLP practitioners will say, "Yes, but behaviour in the Logical Levels relates to what you do." Confused? I don't doubt that.

Let me explain, and I will give you a personal example. I mentioned that I have the professional qualification to practise as a chartered surveyor. When people used to ask me what I *do*, I used to say I am a chartered surveyor. I actually used to cringe, and feel very uncomfortable when I used to say that to people, because even though at that point in my working life I was *practising* as a chartered surveyor, I hated saying I *was* one.

Can you spot the difference? Saying I practise, or work in something, refers to my behaviour. But me saying "**I am** a chartered surveyor" I am referring to my identity.

I was never a chartered surveyor, in terms of expressing my identity. My identity means a lot more than just my occupation, and actually it was a poignant pointer that I wanted to do something else with my life, such did I hate to describe my identity or have people identify me by the work I was doing at the time.

My identity means a lot more than that. My identity is about my creativity, my ability to entertain, my ability to articulate a message and more. So that's why, when I look at this Logical Level (behaviour) I want to look closely at my behaviour in relation to what I want to do, and if it relates to my identity, as a true expression of my identity.

This though should give you a clue about what you want to do, and that you may want to adopt the Cojones Code to get there, however it relates.

So, as they say in parliament, I will refer you back to the answer I gave some moments ago in relation to behaviour: "Do your homework" in whatever area it relates.

Statement 5 – Environment.

Finally, we get to where I left off in Chapter 11, when I was talking about who you put around you.

This level refers to where you are, or whom you are surrounded by. Now, I sometimes like to go to my local coffee shop and have a coffee and work from there. Much of this book has been written there. Why? The environment seems to inspire my 'doing' mode and/or my creativity.

Where do **you** work best? Or, where are you at your most ballsy?

For sure, we all perform better in different settings than in others, either geographical settings or surrounded by certain people, or even things. If you know the where, or even the when, you can transpose that into action you want to take by possibly ensuring the right environment for yourself.

But, as I was saying, if you want to adopt the Cojones Code, the one thing I advise you strongly to do is to have as little contact with the naysayers as you can. They also form your environment. Yes, the people you put around you. Unless you are an old pro at the Cojones Code, and I'm guessing that because you are reading this book you're not, then put yourself in the best settings to be effective.

And if they're family, then politely tell them, or anyone for that matter, that you can do what you want, and **can** and **will**. The **can** and **will** being the pivotal words.

Application of Logical Levels

In summary, the Logical Levels is a model of your way of thinking, and when applied to Cojones allows you to realise where your blockage is. You don't necessarily have to make changes at the level you have the blockage as they all interlinked. But they show you in further detail what you've been doing, or probably haven't been doing, in order to do whatever ballsy thing it is you want to do, or live according to the Cojones Ten Commandments, for an authentic life or scenario that you seek.

When you can look at the different levels, it will allow you to identify underlying patterns, and you can then intervene using some of the psychological interventions we have looked at to unblock them.

CHAPTER 14:

LIGHTING THE COJONES FUSE WITH THE COJONES PUSH

So we've covered a whole range of stuff in the book up to now.

We've covered some psychological interventions, linguistics, Cojones Icons and how we should model them, and the Logical Levels, which all offer amazing insights into how to obtain and adopt the Cojones Code, as well as according to the Cojones Ten Commandments.

But are you still sitting there, or even standing there (perhaps you're on the train and you've not managed to get a seat), and still not pushed yourself from inaction to action? A bit like standing at the top of a bungee jump and not actually jumping off. Don't fret, Cojones isn't about extreme sports. Well it could be, but that depends on you.

In this scenario, in life and across the board, we need that something in our mind that says 'Jump'. Or… 'Jump already!'

Of course, it's the thoughts as we've highlighted that flood in that stop you jumping, and before I highlight what I call the Cojones Push, I'd like to briefly touch on one more thing that often prevents us from doing things. Another one of my titles – the **'Yes-buts'**.

I may have mentioned earlier that I come from a family of worriers. It's as if our raison d'être in life is to worry. If we have something to worry about one day and it's no longer an issue, my family will find something else, and pretty quickly, to worry about.

Oh, before I go further on it. Do you know what a worry is? It's a negative **thought** about the future. So if you're a worrier, then you'll likely be spending your moments fretting about the future. Most of what you worry about doesn't transpire in the end anyway. What a waste of time then. Or, what a waste of the moment.

Anyway, this worry goes further and seeps into other things, it is a restraining factor in adopting the Cojones Code, and it is what I call the 'Yes-buts'.

What are 'Yes-buts'? They are the stumbling blocks that worriers and doubters immediately grab on to when they are faced with the prospect of *being*, *saying* or *doing* something with themselves or their life. Much like waking up in the morning if you're short sighted and quickly reaching for your glasses.

Actually, I used to get up and put my glasses on straight away, but recently had laser surgery, so I don't need to bother any more with glasses. Amazing. How about having 'laser surgery' on your worries?

I have personally in years gone by been a serial 'Yes-butter', finding reasons for not taking action. Looking at what could potentially go wrong, rather than what could go right.

By all means, look at the risks (proper risks) of any serious endeavour, but if you automatically find the 'Yes-buts' and let them stop you in your tracks, then you certainly need to grow a pair and adopt the Cojones Code.

If you are not frustrated with your 'Yes-butting', and you're happy and contented, then that's cool, but often people have regrets if they are 'Yes-butters', and actually wish they had had the balls to do whatever it is they could have.

So, the first thing is to change the 'Yes-but' to a very emphatic, "If so, so bloody what!"

What does that mean? It means you are changing your mindset to the question "What's the worst that can happen?"

One of the Cojones Icons I interviewed for my TV channel is former *Dragons' Den* star and entrepreneur Sarah Willingham. When I interviewed her, one piece of great advice that has worked for her in her extremely successful business career is "What's the worst case scenario?" If she knows she can handle that worst case scenario, she has learned that that's her cue, and if she wants to do it, go for it.

So, in any endeavour across the Cojones spectrum, if you know that the worst case scenario can be handled, and that the positives you seek are attainable, why do you want to look back and regret? I have previously had many regrets and that's been down to my serial 'Yes-buts'.

Of course, when you are metaphorically 120 feet high and supposed to be launching off a bridge for your bungee jump, I'm not going to be there to push you off, but what can really help is to get your brain to start working towards the whole notion of being ballsy, to taking the action you need to, whatever that may be, by engaging your brain in imagining.

Are you aware that the brain doesn't know the difference between the imaginary and the reality? That's right, if you imagine something positive, the brain believes it is the reality, and knowing that, why don't we start by imagining what it would be like to actually have Cojones.

So to start with, and to get yourself to imagine, let's begin by asking yourself the following questions:

What would happen if… ?

Wouldn't it be fun if… ?

Wouldn't it be unique if… ?

Wouldn't it be amazing if… ?

What would happen to my life if I did… ?

Or statements:

If I had the Cojones I would…

If I were more ballsy I would…

If I had more audacity I would…

If I were more courageous I would…

You can literally take each one of these statements, finish them off with whatever you want, and start imagining. Use all your senses to imagine what you would see, hear and feel. Be utterly immersed in the experience.

This chapter could have been one of the first in a way, as it will start to propel you towards what you want, but you can always turn back and look at the stuff we covered in order to embolden you and get you to take the action.

After doing the above, you can play with it. If you want, you can work backwards, you could start from the negative:

What would happen if I didn't...?

Wouldn't it be dull if I didn't...?

What would happen to my life if I didn't...?

Or statements:

If I don't adopt Cojones I won't...

If I'm not more ballsy I won't...

If I don't become more audacious I won't...

You could similarly imagine yourself in 25 years' time, looking back at now, and asking yourself why you didn't...

Of course, you would again need to fill in the space or dotted bit to be more precise.

Some people need to push themselves through the experiencing of pain before getting off their backsides, hence why I have included the exercise of asking yourself what happens if I didn't or don't.

Everyone has different motivators, and of course it helps to know what your motivators are.

Excuse me for going off on a bit of a tangent, but entire books have been written on understanding your own motivators and their contexts. One I recommend is *Words That Change Minds* by Shelle Rose Charvet, which looks at numerous filters we each have in different contexts to understand what motivates us and makes us tick.

By having an understanding of those, it can be useful to apply the appropriate language in order to motivate yourself and others, and convince yourself, or them, of something, or doing something.

Very briefly, three of the many filters within this theory known as the LAB Profile are relevant in the field of Cojones, and becoming ballsy, particularly the following:

Direction Filter

Are you someone who is motivated into action by going **towards** a goal or **away from** a problem?

People who are in the **towards** group in a particular context are motivated into action with a focus on the goal. People in the **away from** group are motivated by a problem to be solved.

Ask yourself what you want in a certain situation, and why that's important to you, or what will having that do for you? Ask yourself three times these latter questions. In answering these questions, notice what you say directly after you utter the word **because,** and you'll get an idea which pattern or trait you fall into, and what motivates you.

If you ask yourself the latter question a few times, you will notice whether you are motivated by '**towards** a goal' or '**away from** a problem'. Once you are clearer which one of these motivates you to the maximum, then you will be better equipped to know if you genuinely want to do something. Remember though it is context specific, and only defines your behaviour in one area, and is not an indicator of your whole personality.

Here is some language too that may well be useful to know if you have a bias for either of the above in a particular context, and which you can also use in dialogue to motivate, albeit yourself:

Towards: Obtain, Attain, Have, Get, Accomplish

Away from: Prevent, There'll not be a problem/s, Won't have to, Fix

This language helps influence you to do whatever you need or want to do.

Action Filter

This relates to whether in a particular context you are either proactive (if you act quickly in a situation with little or no consideration and with little thought) or reactive (where you make a complete study of *all* the consequences and then act).

Now of course, Cojones relates to taking action, so it is a little confusing I know. But both are taking action, it just relates to *how* you take action, in a particular context. Again, if you know what motivates you, you will know how best to take the action, so worth knowing I'd say. And here is some language that may well be useful to know if you have a bias for either of the above in a particular context, which you can use:

Proactive: Go for it. Don't wait. Get it done, FFS (you can work out what this stands for) Just do it. Take the initiative.

Reactive: Now you've considered it. Now you've done your homework. The time is ripe.

Chunk Size

In a context, when you are about to embark on something, do you tend to want to know the big picture or the little details first? Knowing this will enable you to know how to proceed. In anything you want to do, it may be helpful to look at the big picture if that's important to you, or if not, the minutiae of the details.

Ask yourself in a particular context: Do I want to know the big picture or the details first? By your answer, you will understand which is in your bias.

If it is a large project you want to embark on, and can clearly see the big picture, as discussed earlier in the book you will then need to do your 'homework', but in the first instance by seeing the big picture first could well inspire you to 'do that homework'.

There are numerous more 'filters', but I'd say these are the most relevant. All of the above enable you to become more self-aware, and by understanding your filters and biases in a context you will know what motivates you to your maximum, giving you the best catalyst towards action and results.

Socrates (the Greek philosopher, not the Brazilian footballer) said, "To know thyself is the beginning of wisdom." Well how true, and the above allows you to do that even better. If you know how to get the best out of yourself, then you'd be a fool not to do it.

Many purists would say the LAB Profile and those filters highlighted above go slightly against the Cojones Code, which is after all about going for it, but I'm merely pointing out the above theory for your own self-enlightenment, and only if you really wanted to understand yourself further in the midst of growing a pair.

Anyway, back to the Cojones Push. After you have looked at the questions and pondered the answers, how about now going back over some of the chapters if you have time, and if you wish, and applying the questions above in order to motivate yourself and adopt the Cojones Code.

For now, let's take some core elements here, and imagine yourself adhering to the Cojones Ten Commandments. Therefore:

1. Imagine what it would be like saying it as it is.

2. Imagine what it would be like being able to speak without constant fear of offence.

3. Imagine something you'd love to do, and what it would be like just doing it.

4. Imagine what it would be like if you rarely moaned and took more control of your life.

5. Imagine if you could truly be yourself and didn't give a monkey's what anyone said.

6. Imagine what it would be like to throw the dice at anything and just play.

7. Imagine what it would be like ripping up the rule books and living by your own set of rules.

8. Imagine being able to ask for anything, no matter the consequences.

9. Imagine what it would be like to fear no one and put yourself as an equal to everyone.

10. Imagine being a shepherd. A leader. Setting the trends.

You may think it sounds convoluted, but I want you to shut your eyes, and literally **imagine** what it would be like for each and every one of them.

What do you see happening, or hear, and most importantly, how does it make you feel?

I don't know you but I can only assume that if you truly immersed yourself into the world of imagination, like you would when you watch a great film, you would likely feel liberated. You would likely think to yourself 'Wow, that really would be amazing'.

But let's go further. What I want from you, or really you should want it for yourself, is to change the would be, so that you say to yourself 'Wow, that is amazing', or 'Wow this is amazing'. That's right, no more conditional tenses, you are in the now, in the doing realm.

That's right, once you have immersed yourself in experience, now change the would (which is conditional on **if** or **whether** you do something) to 'it is', to present tense, meaning you are going for it, whatever the it is.

By doing this exercise, your brain is opening itself up to the possibility of living without boundaries, or perceived boundaries, and preparing itself, and therefore yourself, for adopting the notion of the Cojones way of life, ie the Cojones Code.

Of course, you will need to find particular examples of where each one of the above is relevant to you, and where it applies, but imagination, brought on by the words in the Cojones Push exercise, means you will already be preparing yourself for the doing, which you previously may have avoided.

By the way, through imagination your brain starts to work out the how anyway, so keep the faith.

Imagination is often referred to as visualisation and is common practice, and none more so than in sport. I never forget the story that Linford Christie, the British sprinter who won the 100 metres sprint Olympic Gold in the 1992 Olympics, used to visualise and mentally prepare over and over what was going to happen.

Or when British javelin thrower Steve Backley was injured and couldn't train and practise used to visualise throwing over and over, to keep his technique and ability ticking over whilst injured. His speedy return to the top after injury is well documented, and he puts it down to visualisation or imagination.

We all have imagination, thus we all have the innate ability to think about what **could or can** happen (not the 'Yes-but' scenario, but the 'If so, so bloody what' scenario), what would happen, and that is the impetus for what will happen, along with the other tools highlighted in this book.

But, to coin a phrase you've already heard from one of my icons, "If you do your homework, you'll pass the exam", or simply put, go and practise.

CHAPTER 15:

WHAT COJONES IS NOT

So you're a changed person now eh?!

You're now a ballsy man or woman, where you live authentically, with vivacity, transparency, audacity, honesty, and more.

You're now someone who says what they think, who goes for it in life, is true to himself or herself, you think outside the box, you ask for what you want, you fear no one, and you're a leader, not a follower. How good does that feel? Great I hope.

Think about it, you now live the life most people would like to have. You're respected, admired, talked highly of, super popular. Well, maybe to an extent, but the likelihood is people may start to hate you, to talk you down. Why? Jealousy of course. Particularly in the UK, where when people reach the top many want to shoot them down in flames, and knock them off their perch, because often people can't handle seeing others change for the better, be successful, or even plain contented and happy.

Why do so many people tittle-tattle about others, gossip, and be excited to tell friends and family about another person's bad news? Well sadly, it's because it makes them feel better. And it is unfortunate that people derive some sort of pleasure from idle gossip. But the truth is that either they have such boring lives themselves, or more likely that they make themselves feel better about their life by belittling and talking about somebody else's sorry situation.

You know the talk. He or she is getting divorced, he or she has gone bankrupt or lost their job, he or she said or did that, the list is endless.

OK, I know there is sometimes some sympathy for others too. People aren't all bad, but many, and I've probably been guilty of it, as have you, even if you like to portray yourself as Mother Teresa, when people succeed become envious, jealous, angry and frustrated. It's human nature. But imagine if we were all able to live in the way I have highlighted earlier, and throughout this book. Would we still be guilty of what is known often as *schadenfreude?*

In case you don't know, schadenfreude is a Yiddish or German word meaning the deriving pleasure, joy or self-satisfaction from the learning of, or witnessing the troubles, failures or humiliation of another. People who experience schadenfreude usually have low self-esteem or self-worth. Seeing another person fail brings them a small but immediate short-term boost. Whereas seeing someone who is successful poses a threat to their sense of self and seeing the 'mighty' fall can be a source of comfort.

So I repeat the question, would the large majority of us, if we lived by the Cojones Code, and had strong self-esteem, experience what is known as schadenfreude? I think not. Or certainly to a far lesser extent. Happy days in that case eh?!

In actual fact then, if we all lived by the Cojones Code, there's the additional bonus that there would be less jealousy, less envy and less of what I call the 'evil eye'.

And if we take one of the lessons I have been referring to, modelling Cojones Icons, learning from people who have stood for something, then we are using others' success as a point of reference, for learning, for bettering ourselves and our own lives. That seems a far better option, don't you agree?

But, and there is a big BUT coming – many of the people who may be considered successful for whatever reason, but often for their financial success, forget where they came from. They become arrogant.

Nobody has the right to be arrogant, regardless of their success. **Nobody**.

I say always judge someone by their inner value rather than their external or even financial worth. Yet, many people who have achieved success become arrogant and obnoxious. I'm sure you can think of some, either well-known or not so well-known people who are like that, and that is where I draw the line and say that is **What Cojones Is Not.**

Here's a quote from Oprah Winfrey: "It's fine to wear better shoes, as long as you keep your feet on the ground."

I love that quote.

Obnoxiousness and arrogance are horrible traits that often behold a successful person. I have said that often you have to 'fake it to make it' or 'act as if'. Well, I would argue, and argue very strongly indeed, that this does not mean being obnoxious or arrogant.

You can adopt any of the Cojones Ten Commandments into your life whilst acting with class, with respect for yourself and others. If you become arrogant, you have lost much of your own self-respect as well as the respect from others.

One of the main derivatives of Cojones is a form of confidence. Confidence is important in whatever minor or major endeavour you are embarking on. But there is a fine line between confidence and arrogance, and if one steps over that line, then the bad feeling from people that I highlighted above will be far more warranted.

I mentioned Donald Trump as one of the Cojones Icons, and many people have ill feeling towards the man for what appears to be extreme arrogance and narcissism, and I would concur. However, I still fancy adopting one or two of his Cojones qualities, but certainly any respect he could and even should command is largely wiped out by his often perceived objectionable and loathsome arrogant behaviour.

So let's be clear on this. Whilst adopting the Cojones Code is about confidence, honesty, transparency, guts, cheekiness, audaciousness, fearlessness and more, if I could add a further commandment for living by the Cojones Code it would be this:

Don't Expect the Norm, But Respect the Norm

That means stay true to the Cojones message of thinking outside the box, being different, and all the above qualities, but respect the norm, or what should be the norm, and that is to have respect itself.

Respect others regardless of what you do, respect others when you go about doing it, and most importantly, respect others when you've done it. Whatever that might be.

Remember then What Cojones Is Not.

CHAPTER 16:

COJONES IN ACTION

This subject is so expansive that I could write a book, studying a number of events and real life examples of Cojones in Action.

I've picked just a few here.

Cojones in Business

Cojones in Sales

Cojones in Relationships

Cojones for Life

You see, Cojones is pervasive in every aspect of life, which is why I get invited to talk on the subject in many areas. I'm going to touch further here on how Cojones, as well as the need for it, shows up everywhere.

Cojones in Business

I actually provide a seminar titled 'Bolder for Business' which looks at how having Cojones is so important in an area of life that is the lifeblood of modern-day human survival – making money. It is a huge subject covering many areas, but let me highlight five of the most important cogs in the business wheel:

Networking

Pitching

Negotiations

Closing

Leadership

Yet again, there are whole books on each of these, but I am going to relate each to what we are focused on here – being ballsy, and yes, you've guessed it, the relevance of Cojones.

Networking

If you are shy and inhibited in any way, how do you expect to be effective at one of the most basic parts of growing a business, which is meeting people and building relationships?

Now, I'll tell you a little story of something that happened to me a while back. I realised that to promote myself and my brand to a higher level, to a bigger audience, it was time to enlist the help of an agent. Someone that people go to to hire me as a speaker and host for their events and needed for upping the ante in the performance level of their staff within organisations.

So, I decided to contact a few of the leading agencies, one or two of them I was already connected with on LinkedIn, and decided to call them direct.

Many people by the way seem to click 'connect' for the sake of it, and not to connect at all really, but to collect... contacts that is, or perhaps to seem important and popular to the outside world. Well ladies and gentlemen, I cannot see the point of that.

I say, if you are going to use these platforms, then great, but you can't beat good old-fashioned contact. So, I called up one chap, by the name of Chris, and his secretary, or gatekeeper as I often refer to them, was insistent on asking what the call was about as she clearly didn't want to put me through. In the end I said my call was about Nigel Farage.

A famous name, and due to that, all of a sudden the MD of this company, who was so so busy, came to the phone in an instant. He'd obviously fallen out of the wrong side of the bed that day because when we spoke and he said to me, "You're calling about Nigel Farage?" I proceeded to say that I'd interviewed him, which was true, and then sidestepped and moved on to tell him what I was really after.

He took umbrage initially due to the level of chutzpah, yet whilst I was demonstrating and practising what I preach about, being ballsy, I thought I would take exactly that tack. In this instance it didn't work, he just decided to put up a wall and be uninterested in me, but many would have thought to themselves, hey this guy is ballsy and tenacious, an admirable quality.

I realise I was using Cojones to quite an extreme level, and certainly to some people I was, but if you are going to be able to 'break down doors' then you may need to employ some different tactics. You can't break down doors with a feather can you? And interestingly, I now do work with the chap, and all is forgotten, as he was just having a bad day when I called him.

Doing what I did does take balls, and I'm not saying this rather extreme approach is for everyone, but this was a case where I was looking to work with a very select pool of people, so I needed to get to them somehow.

In the same way, networking isn't for everyone, as people are uncomfortable at approaching others.

What I'm saying of course is, if you want to meet people, and build relationships, then you are going to have to be able to face your discomfort and feeling ill at ease head on by getting rid of self-consciousness at networking events or gatherings, and getting on the phone for follow-ups (or introductions possibly!). Meeting people takes an element of ballsiness.

Remember the Cojones Ten Commandment number 9: Fear No-one, Approach Anyone. Hopefully you will have picked up the tips and tools for building your balls, so you can do this.

You see, business is, at its foundation, about building relationships, as well as about starting them. How easy do you find it to talk to people you don't know, introducing yourself to people from cold, asking for their card, giving yours etc etc?

Of course, there are many books on networking as there are on sales, but if you haven't got a pair of Cojones, then you will be largely ineffective, and the books will offer you nothing. If you adopt the Cojones Code, you will be laying the right foundation to build your skills and networking ability.

To summarise, and based on what we discussed earlier, let's briefly look at what is needed for the networking side of things.

First of all, before overcoming inhibition and fear, it is important to understand inhibition and fear.

In terms of networking, and many other types of socialising, people are largely inhibited due to judgment. By their own self-judgment, but also, and perhaps more importantly, of others' judgment of them.

Your own self-judgments are your own thoughts. And your idea or perception of others' judgments of you are also your own thoughts.

In theory, if you do have something to sell, and you are confident in the benefits it brings to others (remember people buy benefits), then you should really have nothing to fear, except fear itself of course. Also, I have mentioned, "You wouldn't worry about what people think of you when you realise how seldom they do."

In the scheme of things, look at all the Cojones Icons that I've highlighted and also look at your own. They all have the trait that when anyone's judging them, criticising them, putting them down, they take it as if it's water off a duck's back. Or if they are much harsher, then they just say about these people that they can 'go and fxxk themselves!'.

The truth is that outside people don't care if you succeed or fail. And really, they are often more interested, sadly, in seeing you fall, so why would you give a monkey's about their opinion?

If you look back to the chapter on subjects such as CBT and the Three Principles you will be able to apply the CBT model by identifying the activating event, or the perception of judgment, and be able to rationalise it, assuming you can't just brush it off that is. Or, just see your perception or receipt of someone else's judgment as just another thought, and know it will pass, like the last breath you took.

Of course, there are indeed ways of approaching people, and this is a skill you can learn. I personally like some of the NLP practices on building immediate rapport by adopting the subtle skills of mirroring and matching.

I use an element of chutzpah, cheek and humour to break down walls and get a conversation going, but I guess that I am fortunate in that I am able to get away with it so to speak. You need to find your own style, and your approach is going to be different dependent on the event, be that an official networking event or a social gathering, or even everyday situations.

As I related earlier in Chapter 3, I met a man who is now a client when I was at the urinal answering a call of nature (yes I am serious). He was on his mobile in the next urinal, not only answering a call of nature but answering a business call. When he said goodbye to whoever he was speaking to, I made a comment that his business must be busy! He laughed, and we got chatting, and I ended up doing a couple of talks to his sales team. Now that's chutzpah. That's Cojones.

Are you cheeky enough to do something similar?

I can tell you, with balls you can network anywhere. I did, in the queue at Starbucks once.

As you may have guessed, I have a mischievous side, and standing in the queue where they ask your name with your order, I heard the name of the chap in front. When we got to the other side to pick up our orders, I said to him "Geoff" to which he looked at me in amazement that I knew his name. He said "Yes" and I made out I knew him. We ended up chatting and he gave me his card. We ended up doing some business together.

Now, remember I said that part of the mindset of a Cojones Icon is play. Well, whilst I don't consider myself an icon, I do like to play and entertain myself, and that is what I was doing, and bizarrely, some business came out of it.

I can tell you numerous stories, but the point is if you adopt the Cojones Code, you really can meet like-minded people, build relationships and hopefully future clients. And with the Cojones Code there's no limit to what you can do. Remember, I met my wife at the traffic lights while we were both in separate cars waiting for them to change to green… A true story.

Pitching

This could be over the phone or face to face. Many people literally freeze at the thought.

Yet, in business, the whole point is to make a turnover and profit, and whether you are selling products, widgets or services, you have to have the balls, as well as the prep, to be able to get on the phone and/or present your USP. If you haven't got the balls, then you shouldn't be in business, you should be doing admin, where your role isn't to generate turnover but to keep things ticking over.

To become ballsy at pitching, you will hopefully have embraced some of the ideas and practices this book has highlighted.

This isn't a book on sales per se, but to be ballsy at pitching means 1) being unafraid at picking up the phone, 2) being confident in your product, 3) being able to stand up (or sit down) and talk about your product and 4) possibly being able to create the pitch itself.

Of course, the first foundation is the pitch itself. This should involve a strong introduction of yourself, where you are from (company I mean, not country), and the product. You then have to be clever about 'creating the need', ie identifying the problem with what's out there at the moment, and then informing the prospective client about the benefit to them of your product or service.

People buy benefits, and once you have identified the potential client's *need*, you will then need to convince them of the *benefits* your product brings them in fulfilling this need.

Interestingly, as you may know, I was in hard sales, selling space cold over the phone – possibly the hardest form of sales, where the turnover of staff is abnormally high and new people are taken on regularly because most of those hired can't do the job.

To be good at sales is about persuasion, communication and yes, you've guessed it, a pair of balls. There are many who are actually pretty good at pitching, as they don't have to pluck up any courage to close, but when it does come to closing they can't do it, so here comes the part of selling that takes the most ballsiness – closing.

Closing

My old boss, Trevor (if you're reading this Trevor, you know I mean you) used to have a saying: 'ABC - Always Be Closing'.

Now, whilst I don't totally subscribe to that, as all the other stuff I have and will mention is equally as important, I do understand the notion. You see, ABC is a mindset, and it's a ballsy one at that, in the quest for the goal, writing the deal. You have to do the groundwork, network, research, pitch, negotiate, but if you have the ABC in mind all the time then effectively you have your mind on the goal all the time. You're focused.

Remember what I said about one of the qualities of Cojones Icons? They have focus. In fact, all of them show this quality, and in the sales environment, if you have the mindset of ABC then you are adopting one of the vital qualities of any Cojones Icon, and are that much more likely to achieve your intended goal, and in this case, a sale.

Not only that, I can tell you, in a sales job you are only as good as your last sale, meaning you have to constantly look for the next one, meaning 'stay focused'. As I always tell people, Cojones gives you an edge on the rest, and if you adopt this mindset in a sales environment, you are staying focused, not resting on your laurels or previous successes, but looking at striving for the next one. That's a champion's mindset.

I write this chapter only a couple of days after Rafael Nadal, the tennis champion, has just won his 12th French Open tennis title. An unbelievable achievement. I am sure he's celebrated all the other titles, but then he continues to focus on the next one, and never seems to lose his hunger. What a champion. In a tennis sense, the sport I love, he's got the mindset of ABC - Always Be Closing.

Thanks for teaching me that one, Trevor. It really does resonate in so many senses.

Anyway, back to the notion of closing.

For sure, it is the part of sales that salespeople struggle with the most, and the reason why so many join the hasty exodus out of sales teams' doors, as I mentioned earlier. It's because they can't and are scared to, and therefore fall apart at the final hurdle. Again, in a tennis sense, it's a bit like having match point and falling apart at the most important hurdle, or missing a penalty in the last minute of a cup final. Actually a lot easier than that, especially with Cojones.

Here's a little anecdote. As I was walking out of the underground station a few weeks ago, a guy who was obviously homeless and down on his luck asked me for some money to get the train to the homeless shelter. Instead of giving him money, I gave him my Oyster card (rail pass) so he could get there.

A couple of hours later, I saw him hanging around the high street near my house, asking others what he asked me a couple of hours earlier! What a cheek! But what Cojones he has! I was naturally livid that my kindness had been taken advantage of, but just left it.

A couple of weeks later the same guy approached me and asked me again for some money "to get to the homeless shelter." This time, I reminded him he asked me the same a few weeks earlier. He couldn't remember obviously, but then I said to him, "You have a talent. You have the ability to ask someone you don't know nor ever met and ask them for money. Why don't you put that to good use, like in sales?"

Whether he ever did, despite him telling me that he was putting his life back together, is irrelevant, because what I'm getting at is that this guy was a natural closer, and someone with that much Cojones should not have been walking or living on the streets. A truly great shame.

In a way, the above story isn't a great example, because it would seem he was a professional beggar rather than desperate to eat, but he was still in great need of money, be that for lodging, food or to fund his drink or drug habit.

As per the Cojones Icons' qualities, if you want it enough, you will likely be focused enough, and ballsy enough, to be able to be fearless when it comes to closing. This guy who asked me for money had lost all sense of shame or fear in the concept of asking, which is what Cojones is partly about, and that is not being inhibited.

The boxing legend 'Marvellous' Marvin Hagler said it was hard to get out of bed for his early morning training runs once he was wearing silk pyjamas. If you are mentally wearing silk pyjamas, then it is highly possible that you mentally are not motivated enough to get that deal.

That 'homeless' person was motivated to get money, that's why he had no shame to ask.

How motivated are you? How badly do you want it? Actually, how badly do you need it? If you had starving children at home, how much easier would it be to ask for the deal if you knew it was going to provide a meal for your hungry kid/s? You should be able to answer that – but yes, a hell of a lot easier.

Cojones is a mindset. When I ask audiences to point to their Cojones, I get many women point down below. Hilarious. It's in your head of course, via your mindset.

So, if you want to adopt the Cojones Code and prepare yourself mentally for the best state and psyche for a close, focus in on how much you need and want it. And if you don't need nor want it, think about how bad you would feel if you wasted the opportunity of a deal. How bad that wasted opportunity would make you feel may enable you to get yourself over the line.

One more thing on this, and again, this isn't a sales training book, but preparing yourself mentally also means ensuring you know **how** you ask for the deal. A confident assumptive attitude will mean your language, tonality of voice and physiology will be right as you go in 'for the kill'.

And if you are still saying "I can't do that" you're either not hungry enough or you're better suited to admin work. No shame in that though.

Negotiations

This is an area which takes Cojones of course, and as we know, everything pretty much does.

A classic case of course is at the time of writing the debacle of Brexit negotiations.

Theresa May, the previous prime minister, was at the helm of negotiations. Now, I don't want to get into a political debate with you, but Theresa May always believed the UK should stay in the European Union. Which meant she didn't want to leave, meaning her strength in negotiations was massively reduced.

The stronger your position, the better placed you are to get a deal done and, indeed, closer to your demands.

Most negotiations require an element of compromise, but the stronger your position, the more power you have over your opposite number.

To that end, is it any surprise that Theresa May did not manage to negotiate an exit from the European Union? I would say no. She didn't believe in the process, thus robbing her of her conviction, her strength and power in negotiations, which you would have to assume the EU negotiators recognised all along and therefore have been the powerhouse in the process.

So, you need to have conviction on your side, and even if you don't have the necessary weight behind you in terms of genuine arguments supporting your case, often in the game of bluff called negotiating you need to give off the air of power, and this takes skill as well as balls.

I don't know how to play poker, but for sure from what I know there's a lot of bluff involved, and if your opponent is able to read your bluff, your weakness, you're done for, and if you're playing for a lot of cash, so is your money.

Giving off that air of power is almost as important as actually having it. A top tennis player should never give the impression that he thinks he's going to lose, because he is then showing in the same way a message of fragility and far more likely to lose, as his opponent will smell blood. Theresa May was the same in Brexit negotiations.

I've been involved in negotiations where the odds were stacked against me getting the best deal, but I found arguments to back up my case, and made them convincingly, because I came across confident, 'powerful' and a man of conviction.

If you are weak, then you will get considerably less than you were hoping for in any deal. You need to grow a pair, and fast.

How? I'm not going to repeat the 55,000 or so words in this book up to this point, but to recap here's a summary.

Act as If – As I have just been saying, but in short, Fake it to Make it. Find the arguments that have some weight and express them with conviction. Ensure your body language expresses what you are trying to give off.

Modelling an Icon – Take a look at the qualities of your own icon, preferably an impressive negotiator. Model his mindset, his motivation, his body language, his vocal tonality, and possibly his or her negotiating style.

Do not backtrack: I'm not saying don't compromise, but what I am saying is that if you set your stall out with a force and conviction that puts you in a powerful position, then the moment you lose your bottle and you lower your demand (particularly if you do it too hastily) you will lose face, credibility and negotiating power.

Sometimes of course, be careful not to ask for the earth; I said 'fake it to make it' and sometimes bluff with enough conviction will see you win the day. But if you are in a weak position, and have absolutely no way you can back it up, be careful, as your cards may well be found out at some stage soon. Be a force, but be a credible one.

Of course the above is a tad vague, as again, there are whole books on effective negotiation alone, but if you have no Cojones, you will likely fail, even if you do hold the trump cards.

A good negotiator will have Cojones.

Cojones in Relationships

This could mean any relationship, but let's focus on romantic relationships, as let's face it, without them the world would cease to exist. And sorry snowflakes and PC brigade, I am going to focus on heterosexual relationships, as that is all I have any knowledge about, but I am sure the principles still apply.

So in romantic relationships, what does having Cojones mean?

It comes to the fore at the very beginning of courtship. I mean if you're a boy (and perhaps a girl these days) you need to have the balls to approach someone, engage with them, and progress matters, inviting them for a date etc. To many this is the hardest part. Of course, there's a skill in picking the right moment, what to say to start a conversation etc. But just imagine for a minute that you had no nerves whatsoever. Can you imagine that?

If you were approaching a girl you liked the look of (if there are women reading this, which I hope there are, sorry again, but I'm a bit of traditionalist) and you had no fear of rejection, fear being what tends to stop people making the approach, you would be far more likely to make that first step.

Yes, fear of rejection is fuelled by negative self-talk such as 'I'm not good enough', 'I'm not attractive enough' and so on, but if you could truly banish the fear of rejection the nerves would not be there, meaning you would come across differently, and maybe even enhance your chances of success.

Of course, you may not be someone's 'cup of tea', or that person may not want to meet anyone, or whatever other reason there may be, which may not be anything to do with you, but still, the biggest regret is not to have a go. At least if you grew a pair you couldn't ever have that feeling.

And remember, it is normally better to regret what you haven't done rather than what you have. Actually, better still, to not regret anything.

I know that things are very different in reality, as emotions are at stake, and when they run away with you they get a grip, and you can be paralysed.

First of all, that stranger or person you want to approach is nothing in your life yet, and may never be. The only part of your life that girl is part of already is in your mind, and let's face it, even if you think in a utopian 'that's the woman I'm going to marry' way, or something equally as dreamy, you will have to stay grounded to realise that she may never be anything, so stop enlarging the thing in your mind.

If you do stay grounded, like in sales, that this is just another lead (excuse me for sounding mercenary), and there are many more fish in the sea, you will have gone some way to drain utopian dreamy energy from your mind, relaxing you for being more fearless for the approach.

I'd say some nerves are good, as you neither want to be nor act cocky or arrogant. Here's the thing though, whatever nerves and fear you have walking up to that person, the moment you break the ice the majority of the nerves will have immediately disappeared.

I sometimes do an interesting exercise in my seminars. I get a male and female volunteer from the audience, and get the girl to sit on the floor pretending to be on the beach, with the male imagining he wants to ask the girl he sees on a date. I then get two other volunteers to stand either side of him, each one telling the pretend admirer why he will fail, as if they were the imaginary voices of inhibition and negativity in his mind.

To enforce that, the volunteers both put their arms in front of the pretend admirer whilst telling him he's "not attractive" and "not good enough", slightly preventing him from making his walk to the subject of his pretend desires. Then, as the admirer arrives to where the girl is and asks her a question, or for a date, a coffee, the two metaphorical negative voices (the two volunteers) leave the scene immediately, highlighting that as soon as you *do* what you wanted to do, ie engage the girl in conversation, your negative thoughts that were preventing you doing so disappear.

The exercise is a wonderful metaphor for how our thinking prevents us from doing so much that we want to, including in the area of meeting people, and as I highlighted in the chapter on the Three Principles, it is just thought that gets in the way.

The CBT model means you can train yourself to rationalise your thoughts, but the above is an example where you may not have time to do that, and when you understand that, often the *doing*, meaning the 'going through' your thoughts, is all you need to dispel them.

Regardless of whether the girl says yes or no, you will feel good about having the balls, the Cojones, to do it. Many simply wouldn't have, because they haven't got the Cojones themselves. But they'd love to, believe me. So, tell them to come and see me, or at the very least get a copy of this book!

And then comes more Cojones in a relationship itself. Many people don't have the Cojones to commit to someone and/or to get out of a relationship.

This isn't a book of therapy or relationship counselling, so I'm not going to go into your history to solve your commitment issues or even your fear of leaving, although you can get a good idea reading my chapter on Transactional Analysis, or even better, check out *Know Yourself, Know Your Partner* by my previous mentor, the amazing Mavis Klein. You'll certainly learn a lot about yourself and why you are the way you are.

Now, I've been in many a coffee shop where two women have been sitting next to me, and all they're chatting about is what is wrong with their man.

First of all, come on, haven't you got anything else to talk about? Not only that, if it's so bad, get out. But many would rather complain than get out, as they haven't got the Cojones to take the action, or at the least tell their partner what their issue is and what they would prefer as a compromise. And yes, many who do dump their man or woman walk right into a relationship with someone else just as wrong a match. Again, check out Mavis's book on why this happens.

But once you realise what you are doing, and you've decided what you want, how you like to feel and be treated, you've got to take the necessary action, which often means plucking up the necessary amount of courage. This entails looking at some of the techniques we've looked at in this book, applying some of the Cojones Ten Commandments and simply *doing* it.

One technique I haven't gone into yet, but will do later, and you can read about in many books, particularly those on NLP (Neuro-Linguistic Programming) is anchoring and about mental preparation. This can also be very useful in preparing yourself, your mindset and state for a turning point event you decide you have to expedite.

I will go into this in the next chapter, as I do feel if you haven't come across it you should practise it to assist you in making important life-changing actions.

Cojones for Life

As you can see, Cojones – being audacious, being bold, thinking outside the box, and fearlessness – are qualities that are applicable in every facet of life. I've given you a brief outline in this chapter how it applies in business, and in relationships, but it's more than that.

If you are a sportsman, to be the best, to have an edge, you need the nerve to put yourself at the top level, to give yourself the opportunity to be at top level, as well as to take your opportunity.

As a tennis fan, they say the difference between a top ten player in the world and a player ranked 50 is utterly minuscule. But the player in the top ten, or at number one, has that extra difference that makes all the difference. That's what Cojones gives you.

If you're a politician, to be able to lead or simply stand for something you believe in requires Cojones. To be able to make decisions, and take the necessary action to do what you believe is right, takes Cojones. It may not always be popular, but if you are utterly convinced you made the right decision, your Cojones will have seen you through despite the possible intense criticism.

If you're an actor or a performer, you've got Cojones. Many a Hollywood actor is worried they may fluff their lines or perform awfully. What about a guitarist in a band? For sure they have the thought that they will play a load of bum notes. Or a singer who's worried his or her voice will break at the point of hitting a note. If you are trained and well honed at adopting the Cojones Code, you'll get through it.

That doesn't mean you won't have these doubting thoughts, the fears, but you'll use them for fuel for the job at hand. You'll take the action and see those fears dissipate, or you'll prepare yourself mentally, like training a muscle for heavy lifting, you'll strengthen the Cojones muscle and *do it.*

You may say to me, "But Keith, these examples of high flyers are very extreme examples." I agree, but dilute them, think of an area of your life where you needed, or had, the Cojones quality to *do* whatever it was you wanted to, as the same notion applies, but if you are going to model an icon, then why not? Learn from the best is what I say.

There is literally no area of life where Cojones doesn't show up or isn't required in some shape of form. So, I'm gonna repeat myself yet again: Isn't it time you grew a pair?

CHAPTER 17:

STATE MANAGEMENT FOR COJONES

So, we've talked about the notion of thought via the Three Principles, how many people train themselves to healthier and more effective thought patterns via CBT, linguistic filters via the NLP models, but what about internal state management for adopting the Cojones Code?

NLP claims to own the technique known as anchoring, but of course the whole notion of visual or auditory stimuli to make you feel a certain way is ancient.

I'm a big fan of the *Rocky* films, and many people like me have claimed that after watching a *Rocky* film they feel like going out training, or are simply inspired to do something they perhaps didn't have the nerve to do before. If you're a *Rocky* fan, you'll understand exactly what I mean. For many, it has the inspiring power to arouse people into a certain way of feeling, thus enabling the **doing**!

I can tell you I was listening to music from *Rocky* as I began running the London marathon. That is an example of the power of inducing the right state, and if you want to do something, something that you feel nervous about, fearful of, or anything that takes a bit of a push, having the internal state where you feel effective will help. Learning what stimuli trigger that positive and inspired response in you is well worth knowing, and using it when you need to, at will.

As human beings, we have five senses through which we process information and experience life. Sight, hearing, feeling, taste, and smell. Normally the first three are the strongest in terms of how we experience life and process information.

So, let's think about this, what kind of response would you have if you found a baboon in your bedroom showing all its enormous sharp teeth? I would imagine a response of utter fear.

Sounds crazy I know, but a friend of mine actually did find a baboon in his room when he went on a safari, when he accidentally left his door open. From memory he told me he had a narrow escape and coped rather well, but yes, fear was the immediate response he had when seeing the baboon in his room. That is an example of a rapid change of state, albeit a negative one via a visual stimulus.

If you work well with visual stimuli, was there a time when you had a positive response to a visual stimulus? If it was overwhelming enough, then how about when you simply think about that occasion? Does it induce those positive responses in you? I would guess, probably.

Now, I'm going to take a further guess and say that there have been many visual memories that induce different types of feelings and responses from you. Think of one. Now! As I'm speaking to you! Was there a time in your life when seeing something induced a state that enabled you to do something? Or let's look at it from a perspective of sound. Was there a sound, a voice, a song that induced in you a state that enabled you to do something that you might not have otherwise?

The *Rocky* music does it for me. Sorry to sound repetitive. But there are others too.

If you can recreate that state from a sound, or as before, if you are more that way inclined from a visual of some sort, then that's very useful, and if applied properly can help put you in a Cojones state, and one which will ensure you take action.

So what you need to do firstly is to ask yourself what sort of internal state would be most effective for a certain situation? What do I need to feel like to spark me into action? I would imagine you'd need a feeling of one of confidence, fearlessness, calmness, and even cheekiness, dependent on the context.

Can you picture an event in your mind that induced any of those feelings? How about a sound or song that induces any of the above?

Shut your eyes when you do this.

For the purpose of trying it now, close your eyes and play the song that gives you that Cojones rush, assuming sounds or music is a strong sensory bias of yours. These days you can access music, literally any song you want, on the go, instantly. If, like the *Rocky* music does for me, you know of a piece of music or song that does it for you, immerse yourself in that song, let it arouse those feelings in you, then go and do what it is you need to once you have induced that particular Cojones internal state.

You may say to me, "Yes that's all very well, but Keith, I could be in a meeting for example. I can't go and put on my headphones and listen to music at will." That's very true.

Here's where the tool of anchoring comes in. What it gives you is the ability to set an easily accessible trigger that will induce the same response without actually putting on your earphones.

How cool is that?!

It takes practice, but I've taught it to people going for an interview, giving a public speech, and for other situations, and it has helped them enormously, so this can indeed help you too.

The idea behind an anchor is often said to be connected to the Russian psychologist Pavlov, who realised that you could get a dog to salivate when the doorbell rings. How? By giving the dog some meat on the ring of a bell, thus creating the **association.** Then, simply by ringing the doorbell, the dog would associate the sound with the meat, resulting in the salivation.

Human beings also do things by association, even as early in life as a newly born baby. A baby cries, then the parent picks him or her out of the crib to soothe him or her. The baby soon associates crying with being picked up, and cries with that very intention, and every time the baby cries and then gets picked up, the baby soon becomes a real crying baby, as he or she knows they will get picked up and cuddled.

Similarly, we can create associations for ourselves that trigger the same feeling/s or state/s that we want in order to be ballsy. And what we can do is to programme our mind so that we create an association or a trigger that will set off those feelings. Many people use the classic touching of your forefinger and thumb to programme a trigger that results in an effective state. Touching your finger and thumb you say? Yes, that's right. But you could set other types of subtle triggers, also known as anchors in the NLP world.

Here's how you do it. The trigger could be any time in your life where you've experienced those feelings, so let's just make up a few, but you of course have the freedom of deciding for yourself.

Auditory Trigger. I gave you the example earlier of hearing a song that sets up or triggers an internal response, mine being the music 'Gonna Fly Now' which is the training music in the *Rocky* films. That makes me feel confident and motivated. So what type of music sets off triggers in you? Can you hear the music in your head without sticking on a pair of headphones?

If you can't, go and put on a pair of headphones. Now play the music, notice how it arouses you, makes you feel. Is that the effective state for taking an **action** that takes Cojones? If yes, then when the level of arousal is at its height, squeeze your thumb and forefinger together. After a few seconds of this, stop, relax, and do it again. Do it a few times, as very soon you will have programmed that mere action of squeezing the thumb and forefinger as the trigger that will set your state for action, due to the association of the squeezing action with that piece of music.

In the same way, if you can simply remember a time when a piece of music or sounds trigger those effective responses in you, then you could even programme the trigger that way, as long as you are truly immersed in the reactive state. If you are doing it this way, best to close your eyes while doing it, therefore ensuring you are truly focused on the auditory trigger/state it induces, rather than allowing anything you see to hinder your concentration.

Visual Trigger. In the same way you did it with sounds or a piece of music, you could do it with a visual scenario. As an example, when I see a stream or lake it calms me.

So, when I am sitting next to a stream or a lake, and I feel particularly calm as a result of being next to, or looking at, the water, I set a similar trigger to use for when I want to feel calm or calmer. My association or programmed trigger is stroking the back of my hand, but it can be anything.

Not only that, if you have set an auditory trigger or anchor, then you can still strengthen that trigger by practising it with a visual stimulus, making the trigger anchor stronger, therefore more effective for when you need it. That's called layering as you are building layers to the anchor with visual and auditory anchors.

As I said, you could set any type of trigger, it could be touching your ear, stroking your palm or arm. Literally anything, as long it works and is practical.

You could also try gustatory or olfactory anchors if you have tastes or smells that trigger a strong state for the action you want to expedite.

Start building anchors for yourself, so that the next time you need the Cojones to do something, you can trigger the state you've programmed, and be in the right frame of mind to 'get your arse into gear'.

Happy days, right?!

CHAPTER 18:

THE COJONES TO RISE WHEN YOU FALL

Here we are, nearing the end of the book, and hopefully you've taken on board the need to grow a pair and adopt the Cojones Code for your life.

Like I have mentioned more than once, Cojones is a mindset that is relevant in any and every aspect of your life. In its basic form, the Cojones Ten Commandments, or if you prefer to call it a guide to helping you become an authentic real person, will help you be exactly that. I am sure that by adhering to its messages you will be happier and more at peace in your own skin.

What the commandments effectively say is you're here on this earth for a finite time, so make sure you live it **your** way. They throw away the discomfort of constant adherence to what everyone else wants you to be. They support your right to be an individual, and your right to be a proud one at that. They show you have the right to have a go and feel good about doing so. They tell you that there's no place for moaning and blaming others, that you are accountable, and importantly, they tell you that we are all made of flesh and blood, meaning we all start off and end up in the same place, so no one is better than anyone else.

I would certainly be curious to know if you could come up with a better set of guidelines. I know they are called Commandments, but there are no rules, as of course they are only written to encourage you to make your own!

The Cojones Code also ensures you have the greatest possibility to 'have a bloody go' at anything you want to, because it is your life. Not your parents', not your siblings', not your friends' and not your enemies'.

Yours, and yours alone!

So what happens if you successfully follow these guidelines?

Well, my friend – I hope we're friends by now after all this time together, but it doesn't always work out the way we want it to. As much as living by the Cojones Code will go some way to ensuring you are more real and authentic, whilst most importantly ensuring you 'go for it', life doesn't always end up the way we expect it to.

You can be more ballsy, more authentic, and everything this book encourages you to be, but does it guarantee the perfect outcome? Not necessarily, and if it doesn't, you need to be prepared for that mentally.

If you are not prepared for the outcome of sometimes falling short of expectation, it could hit you, and hard, and prevent you from moving forward on to the next bit of positive action, and certainly hinder your Cojones.

The first thing you have to bear in mind, and this includes all we have covered, is that having Cojones gives you an edge, a definite and definitive edge, but it guarantees you nothing. Unfortunately, nothing guarantees you anything. Except in life the only thing that is sadly guaranteed is, of course, death.

If you keep going you will get somewhere. Where exactly? I cannot say. But you will be on the road, and whilst you may have to change your goals and direction, even slightly from time to time, if you keep going you will reach your destination.

What's most important is of course to enjoy being on the road, the journey itself. That's tough though. I know. When you hit a stumbling block, or a negative, it can really steer you off course, deflate you, meaning you may give up.

I speak with experience in that there have been numerous times that I have had a goal, and the moment I have faced a stumbling block I got deflated and literally gave up the ghost. Actually, invariably, the stumbling block wasn't necessarily there. It was of course my perception of that stumbling block, and of course the fear of future stumbling blocks. That's why I speak with experience that adopting real Cojones is about being able to rise up in the face of difficulty. Being able to run through that wall, which is often only perception anyway.

The first thing to be clear about is that with any project you embark on, success cannot be guaranteed. One of my Cojones Icons mentioned earlier in the book, sports promoter Barry Hearn, claimed, "If you do your homework, you'll pass the exam." But in the reality of life, or even business, you can do as much homework and preparation as you like, you will hit stumbling blocks, and that's when you'll know whether you really have Cojones, and the qualities they infer.

It's great being confident, fearless, audacious when you're swimming with the tide, but when the tide turns you have to show your true spirit, and that's what all those Cojones Icons can do and have done. They stay focused and keep going.

Possibly the most famous baseball player ever, Babe Ruth, summed it up when he said, "The hardest person to beat is the one who never gives up."

You may well get a bit despondent. And you will need to know from the outset that despite wanting to control every situation to achieve the certainty you are after, it's not going to happen like that. The distress that will test your will, and test your Cojones, is indeed the disparity between what you want and what exactly you get. It is rare if you don't ever experience that disparity.

Remember, the biggest predictor of success is persistence, and it is your doggedness, which is your true Cojones spirit, which will fuel that persistence.

Here's another quote by Henry Ford: "Obstacles are those frightful things you see when you take your eyes off the goal."

How very pertinent. You need to keep going as Ford said, keep your eyes on the goal. Except, be prepared to shift the goal if necessary if proper obstacles present themselves, although it may only take a minor shift.

And what do you do when the obstacles in your way shake your confidence, your ability to be bold, audacious etc? You can bring in the armoury of stuff outlined in this book of course.

1. Look at the linguistic meta model of NLP to adjust your self-talk.

2. Rationalise your self-talk using the CBT model.

3. If your obstacles are perceptions, then you'll know perceptions are just thoughts and you shouldn't take them seriously, as healthier thoughts will soon enter your mind – ie the Three Principles.

4. Look at your icons, with the qualities you need to 'go forth and multiply' so to speak. What would they do? What have they done? How have they done it?

5. Keep going and get yourself into the optimum state to take the action that would surmount the obstacle. Once you get over the hurdle, the goal will become even clearer.

6. Use the Cojones Push to put seeds of what you really want back into your head to motivate yourself.

Applying some of the Cojones Ten Commandments can also be difficult when people try to 'pooh-pooh' you and your endeavours, when you say it as it is, or when you set your own path etc.

People, including your family and your friends, more often the most judgmental actually, will attempt to rein you in, because they are jealous of **you** taking control of **your** own destiny rather than doing what they and others say your destiny should be. When this happens, say to yourself very loudly "Fxxk 'em!" That's not always easy because people believe they have the divine right to tell you what you **should** be doing. So I say it again, "Fxxk 'em!" "Fxxk 'em all!"

They are not the ones who are going look back and say, "I wish I'd have done, said, or been this or that." It will be you.

So again, when you meet resistance to being authentic and taking control, and you are finding that difficult, and if saying to yourself loudly "Fxck 'em" isn't enough, then look at some of the models I have looked at, as they will all be helpful to you.

The bottom line is that when things get tough, that's when you need your Cojones. When the going gets tough is the time when you truly know you have grown a pair.

Again, remember, adopting the Cojones Code into your life is not always easy. But if you keep building that muscle it will get a whole lot easier, and if you can do it when you have 'fallen' or taken a knock, then that muscle will be ever so much stronger.

So come on, time to grow a pair!

CHAPTER 19:

SUMMING UP

By now you should be utterly convinced that the most authentic and the most opportunistic way to live is by adopting the Cojones Code. That's right, by growing a pair.

If you do, you'll be very much in the minority.

You'll be able to walk proud of who you are.

You'll be able to stand up for yourself, as you bloody well should.

You'll be able to think differently from the rest of sheepish humanity.

You'll be proud to be yourself. As simple as that sounds, few actually are.

You'll be prepared to have a damn good crack at things that others wouldn't.

You'll be able to brush off demotivation from others, as from your own self.

You'll be able to ask for what you want, and not feel inhibited.

You'll be able to set your own rules, not follow the perceived fixed ones.

You'll be able to do things in the name of play, and not take stuff too seriously.

You'll not be moaning as much about how the world won't shape itself according to you.

You'll not be walking on eggshells when speaking your mind in the midst of snowflake political correctness.

You will see everyone as your equal, because they are.

You will set your own path, and not follow one set by someone else who had the Cojones to set their own.

I could go on and on and on and on. Do I really need to convince you anymore? Actually, if you don't want some of the above, then I would be utterly shocked. Of course you bloody well do.

That said, many don't, as they like the simple life, falling into line with conformity like sheep. There's an argument for that. There's less pressure for a start, and to some extent it would be an easier life, but without Cojones there's no authenticity, no progress and certainly no evolution.

The world and what it has to offer us as we pass the limited time we all have has evolved enormously over the years, with greater creature comforts, greater freedoms (in the West at least), greater ability to communicate (if you exclude the moronic PC brigade), greater choice in terms of food, entertainment. The list goes on, and it boils down to one single facet that has enabled these privileges, and that's Cojones.

I pointed out at the beginning of this book that all the so-called self-help, personal development 'gurus', motivational speakers who tell you that you can do whatever you want in a utopian idealistic way are allowing you, convincing you, to bark up the wrong tree.

Anything worth doing, anyone who's done anything out of the ordinary has had the balls to do it. Not think it, but do it. That's the difference. Yet, all the self-help utopia will tell you is to *think* you can do anything. Cojones and having balls is about getting off your arse, get everything out of the way as you head towards the target. Thinking and *believing* is indeed a vital part, and a quality of a Cojones Icon, but it's a part, and isn't the only quality that's required.

As human beings, we have the advantage over our animal friends, as we have the cognitive ability that allows us the process of evolution and progress. Bizarre that, isn't it? We are called human beings, yet we have enormous power to be human doings.

Really, it is the animal kingdom who are the be-ings, as they act solely according to instinct. Humans of course act according to instinct given to us via the life programming of family and peers, as well as evolutionary and historic programming, but we have the power to **do,** which is what enables us the power to change and evolve.

Naturally, there are negatives to that. Even the Cojones Code has negatives that are abused.

Take the Cojones Commandment Say It As It Is. If you adhere to this in its purest form then you will likely offend someone or many. I'm not saying offend. What I am saying is don't walk on eggshells because of the fear of offending. There are ways to say what you feel in a less offensive or upsetting way. Unless of course you wish to cause offence, and let's face it, some people deserve to be offended.

Or, take the commandment Like Nike, except 'FFS' Just Do It. Again, I'm not saying do whatever you want any time, any place. I'm saying, as per one of my Cojones Icons referred to, calculated risks, and "If you do your homework, you'll pass your exam."

Like anything then, one has to apply common sense to the application of the Cojones Code, whether that means adhering to the Cojones Ten Commandments or modelling an icon. Adopting the approaches of this book and its lessons and messages is powerful stuff. Look at all the people who have and do apply it. But without applying a common sense approach, it can be reckless, even dangerous perhaps.

So, when you apply the Cojones Commandments, have them in mind as guidelines but be smart. Perhaps there should be yet another commandment, saying 'Use the above as a guideline, not the law'. As guidelines, they truly do set the tone for what is possible and what is authentic. That is what you, and I, need to aim for.

When modelling an icon, use their positive **qualities** for the good. Many would say, and I have had it levelled at me several times by audiences, "Why use Donald Trump as an icon?"

The answer is, and above is the clue, you're not modelling the person as a whole, you are taking some of their useful qualities and modelling those. And yes, as my mother always tells me, everyone has some *good* qualities. But again, apply with caution and sensibleness.

I know you will still question the Cojones Ten Commandments, however tongue in cheek they are. Many people will continue to question the whole notion of modelling icons because you still get the wrong end of the stick. Well, that's tough. I really don't care, as I can't be any more clear and reasoned.

Some of the other interventions discussed may be less politically questionable and may be more for you, but I do think everything in this book is relevant, worth knowing about and learning how to implement to some degree or another. The choice is yours of course.

If you've made it this far, then you obviously see some relevance to my message. If you've made it this far, you'll likely agree people should live more authentically, be more real, be themselves and be accountable. That's great if so, because I am utterly convinced that if this is what everyone would want, then we'd all be more real, more decent, less envious and jealous of others, and more effective in this thing we call life. That would be great, would it not?

I will after this chapter highlight some more wonderful quotes that underline the messages of Cojones, but I will leave you with this question, that I always ask:

"ISN'T IT TIME YOU GREW A PAIR?"

CHAPTER 20:

WISE QUOTES THAT INSPIRE A COJONES MINDSET

I love quotes of wisdom. So much as you know can be interpreted by the word, which is why of course I thought it worthwhile to write a book, but quotes are short and sweet, and can be incredibly inspiring.

Seeing that this is a book that talks about a mindset and a way of life, I thought what better way to finish it but with some quotes from people a lot wiser than me that will inspire you, and get you putting some of this stuff into action.

So here are some, in no particular order, followed by my interpretation in terms of the relevance to Cojones.

"I still have my feet on the ground, I just wear better shoes." Oprah Winfrey

I dedicated a chapter to what Cojones is not, arrogance being one of those. We know, if you have Cojones, you will for sure be better placed and equipped to be a success in what you choose to be a success at. This quote just makes sure you remind yourself that regardless of success to not forget humility, and never let success go to your head.

"Experience is something you don't get until just after you need it." Steven Wright

I did talk about calculated risks, but of course, to a degree, anything you embark on will mean hitting obstacles, some of which you would handle better with more experience. Or, you'll make mistakes which with experience you may not have made. Making mistakes is going to happen when you go for it, however calculated you are. But of course, with Cojones, you keep going.

"When you complain, you make yourself a victim. you speak out, you are in power." Eckhart Tolle

Do I really need to be explicit in repeating one of the Cojones Ten Commandments? I think not. But like I say, No Moaning. No one Wants a Headache.

"A decision today changes tomorrow forever." John Di Lemme

*Decisions are a procrastinator's or any self-doubter's nightmare. But if you **decide,** you will likely **do**, meaning things are going to change for you, and possibly others. Actually, have the balls to make a decision.*

"You can do anything if you have enthusiasm. Enthusiasm is the yeast that makes your hopes rise to the stars." Henry Ford

As highlighted in the traits or qualities of Cojones Icons. Makes sense doesn't it?!

"The key to freedom is not to take your thoughts personally." Unknown

As per my chapters on Three Principles and CBT. Your thoughts hold the key to everything.

"The tragedy of life is not that it ends so soon, but that we wait so long to begin it." W. M. Lewis.

I know, because I've wasted loads of it – time that is. Money comes and goes, but time only goes. So with Cojones you will be more likely to begin your life rather than let time simply pass, as it does.

"Even if you're on the right track, you'll get run over if you just sit there." Will Rogers

I, of course, do encourage thinking differently, outside the box. This is important so that you always stay ahead of the game. However, this can relate to complacency too. Complacency means you stop moving. So, indeed, never get too complacent. Pretty obvious really.

"The greatest glory in living lies not in never falling, but in rising every time we fall." Nelson Mandela

Can I really add to that? Only to say read the chapter on Cojones to Rise When You Fall.

"I wanted to change the world. But I have found that the only thing one can be sure of changing is oneself."
Aldous Huxley

This whole book is about being able to change yourself to become authentic and more effective, so yes, do focus on changing yourself, if you feel that is what you want of course.

"The trouble with the world is that the stupid are cocksure and the intelligent are full of doubt." Bertrand Russell

I love this one because I have seen so many successful (financially successful ones generally) people who are utterly ignorant, and simply can't see how stupid they are. But here's the thing that you can conclude from this: these people simply fail to see their own limitations, and that is very often a good thing. This book is partly about seeing past your limitations, so perhaps intelligent people can indeed learn from the 'stupid' ones. Takes all sorts to make a world I guess.

"Why are you trying so hard to fit in when you were born to stand out?" Ian Wallace

I guess I must have ripped off one of my Cojones Ten Commandments from this, albeit unintentionally, as it is essentially saying the same thing: Be You, Nobody Else Will.

"Where the willingness is great, the difficulties cannot be great." Machiavelli

If you check out the qualities of Cojones Icons, you can see that they include being focused, motivated, and having conviction. They underline this quote, and with these qualities this quote comes to life.

"Everything can be taken from a man but one thing: the last of the human freedoms – to choose one's attitude in any given set of circumstances, to choose one's own way." Victor Frankl

Very true. This quote comes from a Holocaust survivor, so he is perfectly qualified to say this. You can choose your own way, as we have talked about for the last 19 chapters.

"No one has ever made himself great by showing how small someone else is." Irvin Himmel

In a world where schadenfreude is so common, in which people are often so happy to hear someone else's bad news, people cover up their own failings by resting assured others have them too, or worse. But with Cojones you focus on yourself, where you don't moan any more, and where you don't have the need to make someone else feel bad in order to allow yourself to feel good. You can do it all by yourself I hope.

"People too weak to follow their own dreams will always find a way to discourage yours." Bob Mayer

Similar to the above. But having Cojones will for sure spark some jealousy from others. I say, let them go and take a running jump, and you just focus on your own course.

"The harder I work, the luckier I get." Gary Player

One of my favourite icons, the sports promoter Barry Hearn, effectively said it when he told me, "If you do your homework, you'll pass the exam." I think this quote underlines this.

"Strength is a matter of a made up mind." John Beecher

Decisions, decisions, decisions. Often hard to make. Procrastination is literally painful. But when you have made up your mind, for sure it feels a whole lot better.

"Avoidance is the enemy of confidence." Ian McDermott

Similar to the one directly above. Making up your mind you will do it, and then doing it, creates confidence.

"Stand up to your obstacles. You'll find they haven't half the strength you think they have." Norman Vincent Peale

Many obstacles do seem insurmountable. With Cojones of course, they are much less so, and when are confronted head on, often they aren't even obstacles.

"Discipline is making the choice between what you want now and what you want most." Abraham Lincoln

One of the Cojones Ten Commandments: Like Nike, except 'FFS' Just Do It! And don't wait until tomorrow, because more often than not, tomorrow never comes.

"I would rather attempt something great and fail than attempt nothing at all and succeed." Robert H Schuller

Sound words, and you'll find that all the detractors who tell you and others what can't be done likely do not possess the balls to do much themselves.

"If we wait for the moment when everything, absolutely everything, is ready, we shall never begin." Ivan Turgenev

This is much about procrastination. So, Like Nike, except 'FFS' Just Do It.

"We must embrace pain and burn it as fuel for our journey." Kenji Miyazawa

You saw at the beginning of this book a sample of my own pain, and actually I used that pain as an excuse to give up on things. But how true this quote is. We should do things in spite of, rather than because of.

"It's hard to beat a person who never gives up." Babe Ruth

Regardless of who tells you you can't, be that others or indeed yourself, remember what one of the most famous ever American sportsmen said here. It will carry you, and motivate you, and he would know.

"The future will soon be a thing of the past."
George Carlin

This is a great quote, merely because it expresses fact, and a fact we all can be accused of forgetting, but one that should give you the fuel and motivation to grow a pair and do whatever it is you want to do.

"We never reflect how pleasant it is to ask for nothing."
Seneca

In a world where creature comforts are so in reach, with choice being aplenty, we are still ungrateful. Not only that. Again, as per one of the Commandments, No Moaning. No one Wants a Headache, when you consider this quote you will realise that actually we shouldn't moan anywhere near as much as we do.

"Whatever you can do, or dream you can, begin it. Boldness has genius, power, magic in it." Goethe

Here is one which is the underpinning foundation of the Cojones message, and if you have carefully read this book, which is all about being bold, you'll heed its message, and adopt the Cojones Code.

"A journey of a thousand miles begins with a single step."
Lao Tzu

Of course it does, and with balls you will take the first step, as well as subsequent ones.

"What lies in our power to do, it lies in our power not to do." Aristotle

Exactly right. I know from experience from the things I haven't done and should have. The buck stops with us.

"If it's going to be, it's up to me!!" Robert H Schuller

As above.

"A smooth sea never made a skilled mariner." Unknown

There is naturally a lot of repetition in many of these quotes, and this one is no different. It's a way of saying you will hit those aforementioned obstacles, but they will merely make you stronger and better equipped to do the job.

"The greatest discovery of any generation is that a human being can alter his life by altering his attitude."

William James

Do I really need to go further? Speaks for itself I would say, particularly when you understand the essence of this book and theories.

"It is better to look ahead and prepare than to look back and regret." Jackie Joyner-Kersee

Like I said, do in spite of, rather than do not because of!

"The gem cannot be polished without friction, nor man perfected without trials." Confucius

Another one about obstacles. With Cojones you will see your way past them, or certainly better your chances.

"Luck is what happens when preparation meets opportunity." Seneca

Again, if you do your homework, you'll pass the exam!

"Obstacles are those frightful things you see when you take your eyes off the goal." Henry Ford

Another one on obstacles. There's a few I know, but remember, it's inevitable we will come up against them, so why not go over the same ground until it sinks in?

"Those who mind don't matter, and those who matter don't mind." Bernard Baruch

I just love this one, as it often works out that the people who judge you negatively don't, or at least shouldn't, matter.

**"You wouldn't worry so much about what others think of you if you realised how seldom they do."
Eleanor Roosevelt**

Similar to the above. Basically it means, fxxk the world, and do things your way. Most people you think give a damn actually don't when it comes down to it.

"Do not go where the path may lead, go instead where there is no path and leave a trail." Ralph Waldo Emerson

As per one of my Cojones Ten Commandments, Be a Shepherd not a Sheep.

"Things turn out best for the people who make the best of the way things turn out." John Wooden

Another great one, highlighting in the Cojones way that making the most of what you have is always the best modus operandi.

**"Everything comes to him who hustles while he waits."
Thomas Edison**

As one of my Cojones Icons said, nothing happens overnight, and this quote says that you have to keep pushing, whilst being patient.

"Someone once asked me what is the hardest part about creating what you want? My reply was learning to stop figuring out how you will get what you want." Jim Rohn

That is, stop thinking too much. Think, plan and do, is to follow the Cojones Code. Overthinking is the dear friend of procrastination, and doesn't bear fruit.

"You have your way. I have my way. As for the right way, the correct way, and the only way, it does not exist." Friedrich Nietzsche

This is so true. And if you are afraid of criticism and negativity, look at this quote. As long as your way is the right way **for you,** *that's the most important thing.*

"When you confront a problem you begin to solve it." Rudy Giuliani

Confront meaning doing. Action. Lack of action is not going to get you anywhere, least not in solving a problem.

"A pessimist sees the difficulty in every opportunity; an optimist sees the opportunity in every difficulty." Winston Churchill

Another one that is so true. In fact, it is through being an optimist in difficulty that entrepreneurs are often born and successful, ie in identifying a need, and finding ways one can satisfy that need, (a benefit) in addressing a problem or difficulty.

"Share your cherished ideas with those who will also cherish them." Alan Cohen

Indeed. Why bother discussing your ideas and dreams with those who will likely pooh-pooh them? Surround yourself with people that will support and encourage you and your ideas.

**"Self-esteem is the reputation we gain within ourselves."
Nathaniel Brandon**

Basically, forget any perceived reputation you think you may have from others. Work on yourself from within.

"Think like a man of action, and act like a man of thought." Henri L. Bergson

Short and sweet is this one, but it underlines many points I have been making.

"To get something you never had, you have to do something you never did." Thomas Jefferson.

And that something may be to grow a pair!

"You'll never find out what you can do until you do all you can to find out." John C. Maxwell

That's right. So have a bloody good go!

"A superior man is modest in his speech, but exceeds in his actions." Confucius

This is just plain good old wisdom. I wish more people could be this way.

"I can give you a six-word formula for success: Think things through - then follow through." Eddie Rickenbacker

What can I say, except… it's beautiful.

"If you do not change direction, you may end up where you are heading." Lao Tzu

So maybe grow a pair, and help yourself change direction.

**"Weakness of attitude becomes weakness of character."
Albert Einstein**

I say, try to be a man of character. Following the Cojones Commandments will enable you to do that.

"Don't judge each day by the harvest you reap, but the seeds you plant." Robert Louis Stevenson

*I've always found it hard, and you may too, particularly if you want success **now**. Doesn't work that way. Patience is key, and as long as you plant the seeds, and water them, the harvest will hopefully come.*

"Will you look back on life and say 'I wish I had' or 'I'm glad I did'?" Zig Ziglar

Think about this one, because it may spark you into action. It may ensure you grow a pair too!

"We are what we repeatedly do." Aristotle

So keep practising what this book tells you, and you will be a person who can do what you want, as well as live authentically.

"To avoid criticism... Do nothing... Say nothing... Be nothing!" Elbert Hubbard

Remember having Cojones will to some degree make you a target of jealousy (from those who wish they had them). This quote says it all.

"Successful business is caused more by mental attitude even than by mental capacity." Walter Scott

Indeed. And this book is about attitude, and adopting one that allows for successful business, whatever that may be.

**"It's not what you look at that matters, it's what you see."
Henry David Thoreau**

That is, our perceptions. Our own thinking!

**"The best way to get ahead is to move your behind."
Unknown**

This one is a bit cheeky. Of course, it means get your arse into gear. Do.

"It ain't about how hard ya hit. It's about how hard you can get hit and keep moving forward." Rocky Balboa

I already mentioned I love the Rocky films. This is a classic quote from the man himself. And it underlines what I've been saying about obstacles, or even worse, taking knock-backs.

"No one ever made a difference by being like everyone else." PT Barnum in the film *The Greatest Showman*

Sums up what Cojones is about.

"If it is important enough to you, you will find a way. If it is not, you will find an excuse. Remember results or reasons!" Ryan Blair

Most of us come up with excuses on why we didn't do something. This quote reminds you of that, and will hopefully motivate you to do the opposite.

FEAR = False **E**xpectations **A**ppearing **R**eal

"As many say, the only thing to fear is fear itself."

"Defeat is not defeat unless accepted as a reality - in your own mind." Bruce Lee

As a martial artist myself, and a big fan of Bruce Lee, what better quote to finish on. We all feel defeated at times, but according to the great man, it isn't defeat until we accept it as such.

So there you have more than a few of my favourite quotes that endorse the Cojones Code.

When you feel unsure about your choices, obstacles, doubts, criticism, etc, just have a read of just a few, to get yourself back on track.

I hope it helps.

ABOUT THE AUTHOR

Keith Fraser is a renowned thinker, speaker and entertainer and the founder and creator of Cojones, the cheeky but wise and profound code for living successfully and authentically.

Keith's entrepreneurial spirit has provided a wealth of experience in professional business, as well as entertaining and inspiring audiences internationally with his straight-talking theories and hilarious anecdotes.

For several years a high-end telesalesman consistently being the leading deal writer, a member of the RICS (Royal Institution of Chartered Surveyors) and a property investor.

With a history of performing and communicating, Keith is a pure blend of wise and wacky, whilst furthering his deep understanding of the art of persuasion and what makes people tick by becoming a Master Practitioner of Neuro-Linguistic Programming, and an exponent of Transactional Analysis under the world renowned Mavis Klein.

Keith is also known for his cheeky and bold experiences, from prank calling celebrities to debating political heavyweights, on TV, radio and in front of live audiences.

As a member of the Chartered Institute of Journalists, recent broadcasting credits include presenting for the first ever Boxing YouTube channel, host of Rock 'n Roll Tennis podcast with former British number one player John Lloyd, and for his own interview series *Cojones Icons* where he has frank and personal discussions with well-known personalities such as Ross Kemp, Nigel Farage, Judge Rinder, Chris Eubank amongst other household names.

In his spare time he enjoys time with his family, exploring nature whilst walking his dogs, playing and watching sport, as well as practising the martial art of Tae-Kwon Do, in which he has a Black Belt. Keith has also performed on stage in comedy and music, as a blues/rock vocalist and guitar player.

www.cojones.biz

🐦 @realcojones

📘 @keithfraserpublic

▶️ Cojones TV